The Charleston Story

Also by JOHN FRANCIS MARION

Lucrezia Bori of the Metropolitan Opera
Bicentennial City
Philadelphia Medica
Famous and Curious Cemeteries

This charming drinking fountain at the corner of Meeting and Wentworth Streets has been familiar to generations of Charlestonians.   Frances B. Johnston photograph, *circa* 1930. Library of Congress.

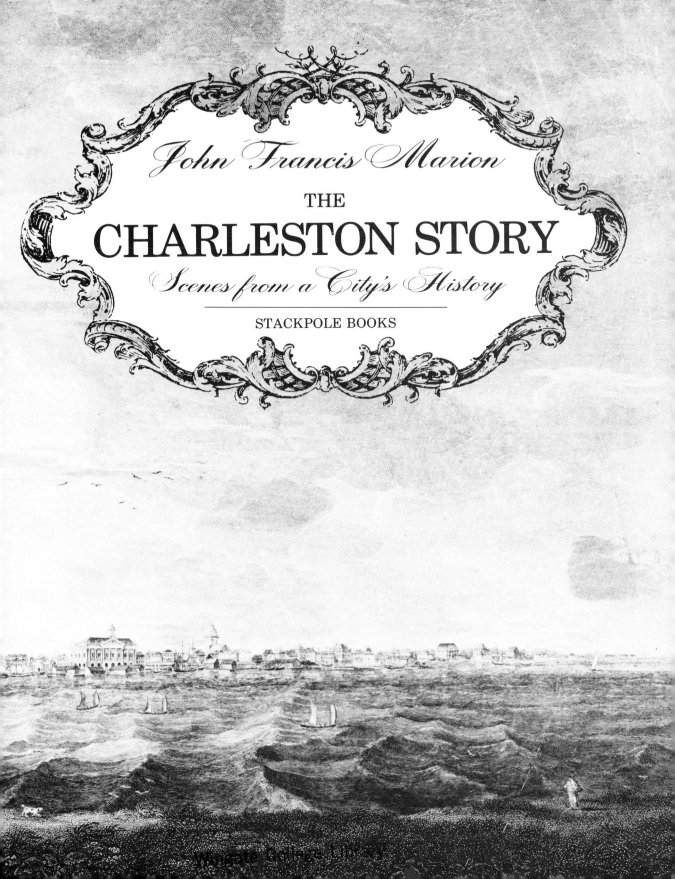

John Francis Marion

THE
CHARLESTON STORY
Scenes from a City's History

STACKPOLE BOOKS

Copyright © 1978 by John Francis Marion
Published by
STACKPOLE BOOKS
Cameron and Kelker Streets
P.O. Box 1831
Harrisburg, Pa. 17105
Published simultaneously in Don Mills, Ontario, Canada
by Thomas Nelson & Sons, Ltd.

Printed in the U.S.A.
Designed by Adrianne Onderdonk Dudden

Library of Congress Cataloging in Publication Data
Marion, John Francis.
    The Charleston story.

    Bibliography: p.
    Includes index.
    1. Charleston, S. C.—History.   2. Charleston,
S. C.—Earthquake, 1886.   3. Charleston, S. C.—
Buildings.   4. Historic buildings—South Carolina
—Charleston—Conservation and restoration.
I. Title.
F279.C457M37 1978   975.7'915   78-13235
ISBN 0-8117-2070-5

PRECEDING PAGES

*View of Charles-Town, the Capital of South Carolina. From an Original
Picture painted in Charles Town in the Year 1774. Thomas Leitch arrived in
Charles Town in October, 1773, and placed an advertisement in the* South-
Carolina Gazette: *"THIS View has been taken with the greatest Accuracy
and Care by Mr. LEECH, who is now employed about painting a finished
Picture from the Drawings already made by him.—The Picture will be ready
to send Home by the next ships, expected from* London, *in order to be en-
graved; and will be so exact a portrait of the Town, as it appears from the
Water, that every House in View will be distinctly known. . . ." Engraved by
Samuel Smith, 1776, after Thomas Leitch, 1774.*   Library of Congress.

For
ALBERT HARVIN WICHMAN
and in memory of
JENNIE MCTEER WICHMAN
and
MARGARET WICHMAN PETERS
of Walterboro, South Carolina
who opened their hearts and their home
to a young soldier

Acknowledgments

I am grateful to a number of people who assisted me in various ways with this book. Albert Hardwick, remembering my love of Charleston, first suggested to my publisher that I undertake it. Clive E. Driver, John Hastings, Priscilla Sawyer Lord, Adeline Pringle Merrill, Miriam Baum Milligan, and Martha L. Simonetti were kind enough to provide me with books which helped in the research itself.

In Charleston Anna Wells Rutledge answered many questions, and Harriet Gourdin Pinckney, the kindest of hostesses, proved to be an invaluable guide to the city. I am grateful, too, to Miss Virginia Rugheimer, of the Charleston Library Society; to Frances R. Edmunds, Historic Charleston Foundation; to the South Carolina Historical Society; and to The Citadel for assistance.

As in the past I am deeply indebted to the Library of Congress, especially to Mary Ison, Jerry Kearns, and C. Ford Peatross of the Print and Picture Department. Thomas Ogilvie of the National Archives assisted me in my search for pictures, as did Marjorie Robertson Maurer of Philadelphia; Sarah Lytle, Director, Middleton Place Foundation; Frank L. Horton, Research Fellow at the Museum of Early Southern Decorative Arts; John C. Milley, Chief, Museum Operations, Independence National Historical Park; Robert F. Looney, Free Library of Philadelphia; Alexander B. Adams; and the New York Public Library.

And for information of another nature I must express my appreciation to the Very Reverend Samuel T. Cobb, rector of St. Philip's Church, Charleston, Caroline Klein of Walterboro, South Carolina, and William Blake Gibson, M.D., of Media, Pennsylvania.

The spectacular ironwork balcony on the Ladson House, 8 Meeting Street, is almost theatrical in its splendor. Frances B. Johnston photograph, *circa* 1930. Library of Congress.

An example of Charleston's superb ironwork. Robert W. Tebbs photograph. Library of Congress.

Authors' Note

Although the emphasis in this book is on the great days of Charleston's past, principally the eighteenth and nineteenth centuries, I have not gone into the long era of Reconstruction or touched on—except briefly—the years between the end of the Civil War and the beginning of World War I. Many readers may wonder why I have not dwelt on the Reconstruction, the establishment of the navy yard, the South Carolina and West Indian Exposition, and other events during these years.

I have endeavored to show the drama of Charleston's history, but I have availed myself of the writer's license to be selective. Since this book was never conceived to be a complete history of Charleston, I have chosen certain scenes to illustrate its progress through more than three centuries. Any omissions have arbitrarily been mine.

Introduction

My association with Charleston is a long one. I first visited the city in the spring of 1926, when my parents took my brother and me there from our home in Charlotte, North Carolina. Although I was but four years old, and I do not remember the city of Charleston, I do recall the Magnolia Gardens, one object of our visit.

In my thirteenth summer, I accompanied my father on a week's business trip, and was permitted to select our destination. I chose Charleston. So, in that far-off summer of 1935, when Charleston was lovely but looked far shabbier than it has since, I was free to wander at will all day long.

My father and I had a point of rendezvous at the end of his business day, but until that time I was an explorer in an unknown sea. For hours I, a solitary wayfarer, wandered at will. I examined façades, peered through iron gates into secluded gardens, gazed longingly at antique shops, haunted bookshops, witnessed a regatta off the Battery, and also saw the points of interest that every tourist sought—the Powder Magazine, the Pirate House, the Pink House. It was an enchanted time for a thirteen-year-old fascinated with history. The impressions have lingered until now.

In May, 1943, as a member of the United States Army Air Force, I was assigned to the base at Walterboro, forty miles from Charleston. On every available free day I managed to be in Charleston. On returning from leaves and furloughs from my home in Pennsylvania, I would invariably arrive in the city at daybreak, hours before the bus left for Walterboro, and before Charleston awakened. At that magical time I

This simplicity of the line in this Charleston home was caught in 1936 by a master of his art.   Walker Evans, FSA, photograph. Library of Congress.

again wandered—Charleston is a city in which to wander aimlessly—and discovered new delights.

In my eighteen months at Walterboro I was fortunate in being accepted by many of the townfolk as a member of the community. Miss Anita A. Bailey, Miss Amelia Frazier, Mr. and Mrs. Alec Henderson, Miss Caroline Klein, Mr. and Mrs. Carl Still, Mr. and Mrs. Albert H. Wichman and their daughter Margaret, and others, told me stories of Charleston and the Low Country, and pressed books on me. The fascination of Charleston—always upon me—began to deepen.

One Sunday while walking with a fellow soldier along Legaré Street, I happened to notice in my guide book that Herbert Ravenel Sass lived at Number 23. I had read his novel *Look Back to Glory*, so with the naïveté and brashness of youth, I entered the garden and asked if I might speak with Mr. Sass. I was told that, possibly, he was sleeping. I persuaded his young son to see if this were so. Mr. Sass, with charm and good humor, aroused himself and came down to talk with a young soldier who was also a hopeful writer. I have since regretted that I did not heed my Walterboro friends' advice and seek out the ancient *Master Skylark*, John Bennett, but following the war, on another visit, I was fortunate to see and hear Miss Josephine Pinckney when she and her fellow-singers (The Society for the Preservation of Negro Spirituals) came to Walterboro for a concert.

So my memories go back a great many years and cover various periods of my life. In returning after many years absence I realized in memory I could visualize Charleston in 1935, 1943 and 1944, 1946 and 1948, so that a continuity had, unwittingly, been established.

There have been as many books written about Charleston as about any American city, yet there will, inevitably, always be more. Its history has been oft told, and it has not necessarily been my intention to repeat this.

In *The Charleston Story* I have attempted through words and pictures to give an overview of Charleston's development, its place in American history, its great architectural heritage, and to picture some of the men and women who have played rôles in its often turbulent history. To tell *all* about Charleston would be an impossibility in a book of this length. And, in fact, much of Charleston's charm lies in its ability—like that of a coquette—to convince the beholder that there is always something new and undiscovered to return to.

For those who know much of its history, these pages may invoke nostalgia. For those discovering for the first time its infinite charms, may you—as I have—find the enchantment enduring.

John Francis Marion

Philadelphia
April 16, 1978

A quiet corner of Charleston with only a cat to invade its peace.   Marjorie R. Maurer photograph.

*"Roo-Roo-Roarey." A young chimney sweep circa 1900. The call was given by
the sweep once he had completed his job and emerged on the roof.* George W.
Johnson photograph. Print and Picture Department, Free Library of Philadelphia.

The Charleston Story

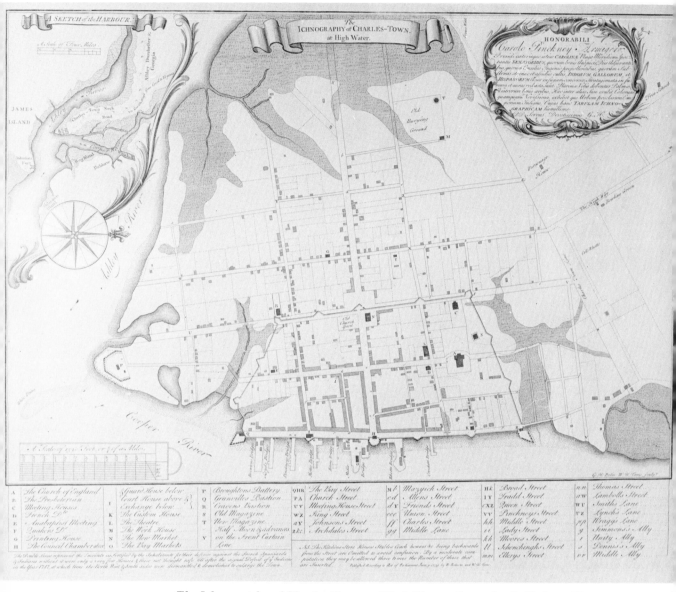

The Ichnography of Charles-Town at High Water, drawn by G. H. (possibly George Hunter, a surveyor), dedicated in Latin to Charles Pinckney, and engraved by W. H. Toms. Published according to Act of Parliament, June 9, 1739, by B. Roberts and W. H. Toms. Shown are the limits of the original fortified town, and identified are public buildings. The drawing was designed to act as a key to the Roberts-Toms engraved view of Charles Town published the same year. Courtesy, Museum of Early Southern Decorative Arts, Winston-Salem, N.C.

CHARLESTON, more than any other American city, retains what at first glance seems to be a European character. Closer examination dispels the illusion for it is soon apparent that this is in reality a distinction of Caribbean origin, with layers of European culture imposed on it: English, French, Spanish, German, Swiss, Santo Domingan. It is this amalgam, together with the Negro culture from Africa, which gives Charleston its own unique and, at times, exotic flavor.

Its location—Old Charleston is situated on a small peninsula of land between the Ashley and Cooper Rivers—provided a remoteness that later developed into exclusiveness and, although a port city, Charleston retained and nurtured its own character because of this relative isolation it enjoyed and continues to enjoy.

Because of its exposure on this tongue of land, and its proximity to the sea, Charleston is blessed with great color. When there is sun, Charleston is splashed with it. When the sea rages beyond the bar, darker colors highlight its buildings and dramatize the city's façades and walls. While not a city of changing moods—its surface has a deceptive calm—it is one given to a variety of colors. Perhaps this since the beginning has been one of its attractions for artists.

For a city more than three hundred years of age—it was founded in 1670—Charleston shows few signs of the ravages of time, or for that matter of the elements that have continually assaulted it. One has dealt gently with it, the other at times harshly, but Charleston has always prevailed. Time has mellowed it beautifully, and its spine has been stiffened by earthquakes, cyclones, tidal waves, fire and water.

DuBose Heyward in *Porgy* called it "an ancient beautiful city that time had forgotten before it destroyed." Robert Molloy, another native son who wrote of his city with great affection, said: "Survival—perhaps that's the one word that, more than any other, explains the city." And the historian E. Milby Burton carried this even further: ". . .this beautiful city, whose charms are now the only defense she needs."

No determined hour is better than an other for discovering Charleston, but it is suggested that the earlier ones are those in which discovery should be undertaken. Charleston, like its antecedents in the Antilles, is controlled by weather. The cool hours of the early morning, when the city is awakening, are magical: that time before shutters are thrown back, the gates from the gardens first opened, and the sounds of feet quietly moving along the old pavements. Then the bells of St. Michael's—each cluster distinctive—chiming the morning

Tower of St. Michael's Church, circa *1751-1761. The church bears a passing resemblance to St. Martin's-in-the-Fields in London. During the eighteenth century when the alarm was raised to warn citizens of fire, a lantern would be hung from St. Michael's pointing in the general direction of the blaze.* Marjorie R. Maurer photograph.

St. Philip's steeple. Marjorie R. Maurer photograph.

hours, and the birdsong in the old gardens, are the sounds most often heard.

It is in the morning that Charleston appears to the beholder to be a setting for some long-gone ante-bellum operetta: the overture is finished, the curtain has been raised, and all is still while the audience waits with breathless expectation for the first action to begin. It is then that Charleston seems to be, in E. T. H. Shaffer's words, "a city of drifted yesterdays."

CHARLESTON'S story is an oft told one, for like countless old cities it has from the beginning attracted its chroniclers. The first attempt at colonization of South Carolina was by the Spanish who controlled Florida and much of the Caribbean. A settlement near the mouth of the Santee River was made by the Spanish in 1526, and by 1540 it is recorded that Hernando De Soto crossed the Savannah River and reached Silver Bluff. In 1562 the French under Jean Ribaut made their way to Port Royal and built a settlement on Parriss [sic] Island. The name Carolina was bestowed on the new settlement in honor of their king, Charles IX, by the French.

Although Spanish colonization of the New World had been vigorous since 1519 when Hernando Cortez opened Mexico, the French concentrated their major efforts on the Canadian wilderness and a few islands in the Caribbean. The English, having carved out a foothold in what is now the United States, were anxious to extend their sphere of influence in this rich, virgin world. The great explorations of the Elizabethans, which continued into the reigns of the early Stuarts, languished somewhat during the stewardship of the Cromwellian republic, but with the ascension of Charles II, the recalled Stuart monarch, English eyes again looked westward.

In 1663 eight men were named Lords Proprietors of a

vast domain which stretched from the southern boundary of Virginia to the mouth of the St. John's River. Their names are still familiar in Charleston and the surrounding countryside: Anthony Ashley Cooper, first Baron Ashley and later first Earl of Shaftesbury; the Duke of Albemarle, formerly General George Monk; the Earl of Clarendon, historian and father-in-law of the Duke of York, later James II; the Earl of Craven; Lord Berkeley; Sir William Berkeley; Sir John Colleton and Sir George Carteret. This decision on the part of the worldly Stuart king was the first visible act in the founding of Charles Town.

Eight years later Sir John Yeamans was commissioned as governor of South Carolina. Soon afterward two fearless and highly important men in the life of the colony, and of Charleston, entered on the stage of the drama then being

Fort Sumter can be seen on the horizon as this family group pauses in its promenade on the Battery in 1912. Detroit Publishing Company photograph. Library of Congress.

unfolded. They were Robert Sandford and Henry Woodward. Sandford explored the region, but Woodward, a surgeon, made a gesture that was remarkable for its time: he remained behind in the wilderness to learn the Indian language—a decision which would reap rich rewards for the colony.

The crucial year, 1670, saw the first colonists arrive on the *Carolina* and the *Port Royal*. The crowded ships put in first at Bull's Bay, twenty miles north of what is now Charleston harbor, but soon afterward found their way to the first settlement in Charles Town—at Albemarle Point on the Ashley River, opposite the peninsula on which the old city of Charleston now stands. When the first men and women set foot on Albemarle Point the Charleston Story began.

WHEN the two barques sailed into Charles Town harbor, the rivers we now know as the Ashley and the Cooper were known as the Kiawah and the Wando, named so by the Indians who inhabited the land. Geographical names, too, were altered. In time Albemarle Point, after it was abandoned for the peninsula, was called "Old Town Plantation." The present site of the city was named Oyster Point before being designated Charles Town in honor of Charles II.

Established as a County Palatine, a frontier province, Carolina's charter from the King was further added to by the philosopher John Locke, whom Lord Ashley asked to assist him. Locke's "Fundamental Constitution" enlarged and added to the statutes of Charles II by providing for a proposed nobility "in order to avoid a too numerous democracy." The titles Landgrave and Cassique (for duke and earl) were bestowed on those, respectively, with forty-eight thousand and twenty-four thousand acres. Those with twelve thousand acres were made barons. The charter of 1665 authorized the Proprietors "to erect. . .cities, burroughs, towns, villages, . . .and to grant letters or charters of incorporation."

THE first years for the 160 settlers, several of whom were women, were difficult because of the proximity of the forests and the Indians, the constant danger of attack by the Spaniards based in Florida, the difficulty in obtaining food (each settler was once reduced to one pint of peas a day), and the low, swampy, humid land which was alien to them.

"Proprietary interests," Carl Bridenbaugh writes, "ever watchful for returns from an investment not yet proved profitless, dictated the founding of a settlement at Albemarle Point . . .but fear of the Spaniard and the 'sickliness of the coast' led ten years later to its transfer to the tongue of land between the Ashley and Cooper Rivers, where it received the royal name of Charles Town. Here a fine harbor behind Sullivan's Island fostered exportation of the exotic produce of this semitropical land."

Several years later Lord Ashley, with the wisdom of a true proprietor, instructed the Governor that the new town in the wilderness should have 120 squares, each of 300 feet. He further directed that

it is necessary that you lay out the great Port Town into regular streets, for be the buildings never soe meane and thin at first, yet as the town increases in riches and people, the voyde spaces will be filled up and the buildings will grow more beautyfull. Your great street cannot be less than one hundred or six score broad, your lesser streets none under 60, your alleys 8 or ten feet. A Pallisado round the Towne with a small ditch is sufficient Fortification against the Indians. There is a necessity that you leave a common round the Towne soe that noe Enclosure may come nearer that the 3rd part of a mile to the Pallisado. . . .

Charles Town's final plan, like Philadelphia's, was a gridiron pattern, "a narrow trapezoid four squares long by two squares wide, fronting on the Cooper River."

In the decade between 1679 and 1689 the number of ships arriving in Charles Town harbor was great and settlers were attracted to the colony from England, Barbados (settled in 1627) and other Caribbean islands. Four slaves did arrive on the ships in 1670, but the first Negro slaves imported by Gov-

An Exact Prospect of Charles Town, the Metropolis of the Province of South Carolina. Engraved for the London Magazine, *1762.*   Library of Congress.

ernor Yeamans, because they were accustomed to labor under tropical conditions, were from Barbados. In 1678 Edward Middleton emigrated from Barbados and the following year Thomas Drayton and Robert Daniel—all to play prominent roles in the Charleston Story—arrived to settle here.

In 1680 the population rose from approximately seven hundred (and in that year one hundred houses were built) to nine hundred five years later, reaching eleven hundred in 1690. One of the earliest protections Charles Town had was a wall, west of the present Meeting Street. A gate and a draw-

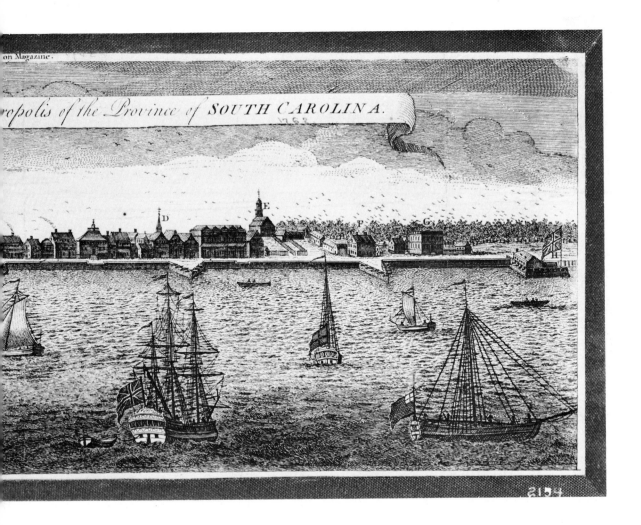

Looking toward the Battery on Meeting Street in 1865. St. Michael's Church, its portico and tower, dominate the desolate scene. Library of Congress.

bridge, reminiscent of the older towns and cities of Europe, led to the country beyond. It was in this period, too, that the first St. Philip's Church was built (1682) on the site where St. Michael's now stands, and the Presbyterians erected (1685) a "White Meeting House," which eventually gave Meeting Street its name. Between 1680 and 1686 the Huguenots— about 450 of them, among them Daniel Huger—joined the thriving town. The mélange of voyagers to Charles Town eventually included English, Scots, Irish, Dutch, Swiss and Belgians, in addition to Huguenots and Quakers.

After 1695 there were no large immigrations and by 1700 there was a population of five thousand within a few miles of the town, and the streets reached from river to river. Relations with the Indians were cordial—a legacy of Henry Woodward—and "most families kept an Indian, who for a mere trifle would supply a household of twenty people with an ample quantity of game, venison, turkey, ducks, etc."—a custom which lasted until the Revolution, and in certain cases even later.

DURING the period from 1670 to 1690 Charles Town had no real municipal government, the rules for the town, church and colony originating in the Assembly, and Charles Town's failure to solve its problems as promptly as the towns in the north—Philadelphia, New York, Providence and Boston—may be laid to just this absence of effective and unified local government.

There were fortifications on three sides to protect the colonists, but these necessarily restricted growth outside the town limits, and until 1717 there were very few houses built beyond the palisades. In fact, at the end of the seventeenth century Charles Town was scarcely a town at all. In essence it was a mere village, which had evolved from a wilderness settlement to become a tidy little seaport. In town there grew a vital commercial society; Charles Town's life blood has always been commerce. Before 1710 this activity consisted largely of exporting pork, corn, certain naval stores and lumber to Barbados, and deerskins to England.

Dr. Henry Woodward, the surgeon who learned the ways and language of the Indians, made another even greater contribution to his adopted land. It is said that in the 1680's he was given a sack of rice by Captain John Thurber. Rather than cook it, as most would, Woodward planted it and thereby founded the rice industry in America. It was South Carolina's and Charles Town's first great exportable crop.

Charles Town was, from the beginning, the center of the Indian trade and traders pushed into the wilderness, gradually extending the frontier hundreds of miles inland. The Carolina coastal land, dotted with inlets and bays and laced with small streams and rivers, was ideal as a highway from the sea. Canoes and periaugers silently wound their way from the tidewater to the headwaters of the streams and rivers. At the point where waterways ceased to be navigable, the pack horse took over.

Labor was scarce in the early years and, because there was no system of apprenticeship as we now understand it, bounties were offered to attract workmen. There were other problems facing the young village-cum-town: in 1684 the Proprietors were misinformed and told that Charles Town lacked good water. Those ruling from London suggested the town be shifted to a new location. Actually, it was soon settled that Charles Town had excellent water because of the geological formation of the land. To everyone's relief—especially the Proprietors in faraway England—it was found wells needed only to be dug about fifteen feet in order to funnel a pure and continuous supply.

The low-lying country presented its own health problems. A "general sickness" developed as early as 1685, which was in part blamed on the "nasty keeping of the streets." This led to yet another consideration of a change of location; the Proprietors did not consider Charles Town "a proper place for a seat of government." As time passed the planters either left their plantations for Charles Town, or went to higher country, in times of fever and sickness. By 1690 Charles Town had in residence four physicians to look after the health of its growing population.

T HE dawn of a new century has always brought man, with his constant awareness of time and its passage, to a point where he moves forward, hoping for accomplishment in the *nouveau siècle* ahead, leaving the experiments, mistakes and disappointments of the century just past to history. Although Charles Town was to flourish in the first sixty years of the nineteenth century and bring a distinct culture, architecture, way of life, and great wealth to the American scene, it was perhaps the eighteenth century that was its time of greatest glory, its apogee. It was surely its period of greatest growth.

Behind the young village on the peninsula with its hastily built houses, primitive streets and infant economy lay the original wilderness settlements. In the early years of the eighteenth century Charles Town experienced growing pains and it grew, albeit slowly, with purpose. There was a ruling class even then, a hierarchy composed principally of emigrant planters from Barbados, the English and Huguenots. This aristocracy—an oligarchy—is traceable from those who then controlled the community to the ruling families of today. More than one historian has pointed out that prior to 1700 there were living in Charles Town the Amorys, Bulls, Harlestons, Manigaults, Mazycks, Pinckneys and Rhetts. By 1710 Jonathan Amory, Colonel William Rhett and Thomas Pinckney were equally prominent politically and commercially, and Arthur Middleton, John Barnwell and Ralph Izard had assumed their roles as influential planters. Most of the names of this privileged society remain in Charleston today, if not always in evidence to the beholder's eye, at least familiar to the

Charlestonian knowledgeable about genealogical and marriage lines, especially on the distaff side.

While the population had reached eleven hundred in 1690, by 1700 it was recorded at about two thousand and a decade later increased by another thousand. In 1720 it reached approximately thirty-five hundred. This rise in the population enabled the village to begin to take on the aspect of the town. Charles Town would probably have grown at a greater rate but for its control by the Assembly, and the lack of local government. Early on there developed a rivalry between the leaders of the town and those planters living in baronial splendor in the country beyond. It was simply a case of the planters' desire to subordinate the interests of the commercial princes in town to their agrarian ones. Although the citizens of Charles Town accounted for over half of the population of the province of Carolina in 1720, they were permitted only four representatives out of thirty in the Commons House. The balance scales were bound to shift in Charles Town's favor; it was only a matter of time.

While early Charles Town fought the demagogues in the Assembly, it also had to contend with the elements at hand. A hurricane of great force devastated the town in 1713, demolishing homes, wharves and warehouses, and uprooting trees. It was a crucial moment in Charles Town's early life for trouble was brewing among the Indians and would soon (1715) bring about the Yemassee War. This outbreak of hostilities brought a movement to the town of refugees from the country regions and the trade in skins and furs languished. In Charles Town, feeling the bite of wartime economy, taxes rose, prices soared and the colony suffered accordingly.

The hurricane, and earlier a storm in 1699 and the fire of 1698, left housing at a premium. In the thirty-year period—from 1690 to 1720—Charles Town doubled its number of buildings, and there was a rash of construction. However, to assure that such calamities did not leave it in a similar condition again, legislation was enacted that all homes were to be built of brick. It was the beginning of the use of that material—although many dwellings were still constructed of

William Pinckney Shingler House at 9 Limehouse Street was built in 1858. HABS photograph by Louis I. Schwartz, 1963. Library of Congress.

East Broad Street in 1906, with the Exchange shown at the foot of the street. Broad Street, the scene of Charleston's financial district, houses many of the city's banks and law offices. Detroit Publishing Company photograph. Library of Congress.

The brickwork in Charleston houses with the passage of years achieves a patina all its own. An excellent example of this is the Alfred Hutty House, 46 Tradd Street. Frances B. Johnston photograph, *circa* 1930. Library of Congress.

cypress and mahogany—and there was a new look of prosperity to the town.

As early as 1701 street names began to be in use—Broad Street, Tradd Street and The Bay (although just a few years before, in 1698, none had an official name), and by 1720 all streets within the original trapezoid seem to have been given names by which they are now called. We do know that between 1692 and 1701 cedar, cypress and pine trees were planted on the main road from town.

The Huguenot Church, Queen and Church Streets, circa 1844-1845. The first Huguenot church was built in 1767, and survived until 1796. A second was erected in 1800, but closed twenty-three years later. The present edifice, de-signed by Edward Bricknell White (1806-1882), was completed by May, 1845. U.S. Bureau of Public Roads photograph in the National Archives.

Early trade was principally between Charles Town, England and Barbados, and by 1710 it extended to other parts of the West Indies and even to the Dutch colonies in South America. Charles Town, in many ways a closer relation to the islands of the Caribbean than to the mother country, began to receive shipments from, and send others to, Antigua, St. Christopher (St. Kitts), Nevis, Montserrat and even the Bahamas. Staves, hoops, shingles, pitch, tar, beef, pork and rice (beginning its career as a staple), tallow, butter and peas were exchanged for rum, sugar, molasses, cotton and salt. And slaves continued to arrive from Barbados and Jamaica. Charles Town-owned ships brought back manufactured goods from London and Bristol, and, as a port of call, stopped at Lisbon for casks of madeira and port that were the pride of every gentleman's wine cellar. In 1720 it was reported "nearly 200 sail of all sorts. . .were freighted behind Sullivan's Island for the export trade."

Although the Church of England represented the established religion (the first law passed by the Assembly established it throughout the colony), Quaker meetings began in 1682, the year William Penn's *Welcome* anchored in Philadelphia, and the Huguenots established the faith of John Calvin in 1687. Folk from the outlying country arrived for services at St. Philip's by canoe and periauger, and the Sabbath meetings in some ways took on the aspect of a social gathering.

However, all was not simple concord in the small town. Dissenters found they could only secure the toleration granted by the Carolina charter by struggling against the Establishment. In 1690 a group of New Englanders built an edifice on the site now occupied by the Circular Church. By 1699 there were some 195 French Huguenot families in the port. That same year a Baptist congregation was formed, and the Society of Friends acquired property and erected a small meeting house (regular meetings soon fell off and were not revived until 1716). "Episcopacy flourished" and a new St. Philip's rose in 1701, only to be replaced by a still larger one after 1715. "St. Philip's enjoyed the support of the Governors and most of the prominent men, such as Colonel Rhett, Alexander Paris, William Gibbons, John Bee and Jacob Satin."

Friction between the Huguenots and the Anglicans developed in the first years of the eighteenth century. The clash became a bitter political struggle, but after following appeal to higher authority in England the objectionable laws were repealed. Many Huguenots went over to the Church of England, and passions cooled when the Huguenots threw off their allegiance to France and declared their espousal of England.

It was not until 1750 that the Sephardic Jews organized Congregation Kahal Kadosh Beth Elohim, although Jewish pioneers settled here early. The first mention of a Jew appears in 1695.

Education was available at the Congregationalist School (established in the 1690's), where Matthew Bee taught until the yellow fever carried him off in 1699, and about 1711 St. Philip's parish established a Latin School under the direction of the Reverend William Gay. The wealthy, of course, sent

Gravestone with its inscription in Latin of the Reverend Nathan Bassett in the Round Congregational Churchyard.   Mary C. Means photograph.

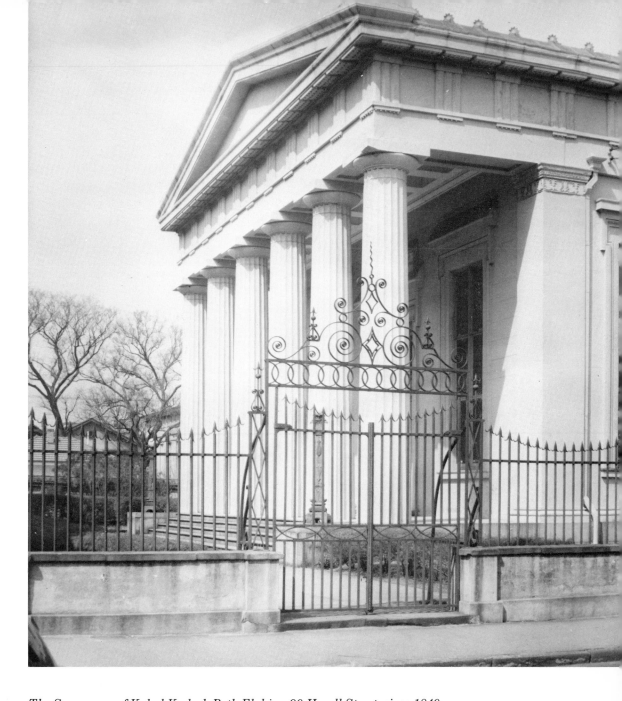

The Synagogue of Kahal Kadosh Beth Elohim, 90 Hasell Street, circa 1840-1841. Remembered as "the Cradle of Reformed Judaism in America," the congregation dates to 1750 (the first Jew recorded in Charleston appears in 1695). The first synagogue of this congregation was built in 1794 and destroyed in 1838. The present building is the second oldest synagogue in the United States. Robert W. Tebbs photograph, 1941. Library of Congress.

Bird's Eye View of Charleston, 1872. Drawn and published by C. Drie.
Library of Congress.

their sons to England and those who pursued law studied at the Temple. And, about 1700, remarkably soon for the young colony, the Assembly passed "an Act for Securing the Provincial Library at Charleston, in Carolina," with Dr. Bray, the Anglican minister, as librarian.

ONE must remember that the Charleston we see today—elegant, pristine, as well cared for as a demimondaine—was not the Charles Town of the early eighteenth century. In 1702 a system was set up to deliver and receive mail from northern towns, and when this foundered for lack of traffic, Charles Town was assured of contact with its neighbors by the ships and packets plying the coast. Pirates brought their money to town and spent it freely, but as in any seaport "the streets. . .were. . .filled with brawling sailors, whose favorite sport was beating. . .the watch."

This situation led in 1700 to a seven o'clock curfew. When the bell tolled, all seamen were to be aboard ship for the night, and "all stray mariners found in town after that hour" were incarcerated in the guard house (established as a place of detention in 1701). The watch—so belabored by the seamen—was noted (in 1709) to be irregular. The Assembly issued a warning that "if not duly taken care of. . .now in this time of [Queen Anne's] war and. . .danger, may be of fatal consequences and the ruin of this flourishing town." Subsequently, an armed watch of one hundred men was ordered to patrol the town nightly.

The obstreperous tars were not the only denizens of the dark. Slaves were caught pilfering "at unreasonable hours of the night" and as early as 1698 the watch was instructed to watch for all such offenders. All was not well on another level, too, for "many women of ill fame, and outcasts from Newgate [in London], approached men openly on the streets at night."

No city in the United States has a more romantic association with pirates and piracy than Charleston, which was close to the Spanish Main and Caribbean Sea, the principal scene of operation in the seventeenth and eighteenth centuries for those brigands of the sea. The Pirate House, a reminder of these daring, wicked, yet fascinating men, still opens its door to the twentieth-century wayfarer in search of mementoes of its inhabitants.

No pirate possessed more glamour than Stede Bonnet, the notorious "Gentleman Pirate." None was more feared than Edward Teach, or "Blackbeard." The latter captured several Charlestonians, among them Samuel Wragg, a member of the Council, and his son, and used them as pawns in bargaining for medical supplies. Either the medications were his or the heads of Wragg and the others would be presented to the Council.

Colonel William Rhett, a soldier who had often proven himself in the past, put to sea with the *Henry* and the *Sea Nymph* in search of Blackbeard. In a crucial engagement which forever broke the domination of the pirates, the *Royal James*, manned by the buccaneers, was vanquished by the Charles Town vessels. Much to their astonishment the victors found that they had not captured Blackbeard, but Stede Bonnet!

Rhett returned Bonnet and his crew to Charles Town in irons, only to find, because there was no jail, that there was no place large enough in which to keep them. Most of his men were locked in the watch house, but Bonnet and two of his company were kept under guard at the home of the Marshal.

Bonnet, accompanied by his sailing master, Herriot, managed—disguised in women's clothing—to escape to Sullivan's Island. While one group of Charlestonians were scouring the "dense growth of stunted live-oak and myrtle [that]

A View of Charles Town, the Capital of South Carolina in North America. Engraved in 1768 by Pierre Charles Canot (c.1710-1777) from an original painting by Thomas Wellish (then) in the Collection of Mr. John Bowles. London. Printed for John Bowles at No. 13 in Cornhill, Robt. Sayer at No. 33 in Fleet Street, Thos. Jefferys at the Corner of St. Martins Lane in the Strand, & Carington Bowles at No. 69 in St. Pauls Church Yard. Library of Congress.

lay close and confusedly together," Governor Robert Johnson, by a ruse, cleverly hemmed in—between the *Sea Nymph*, the *Royal James*, and Charles Town itself—a pirate vessel, the *Eagle*, threatening the harbor. A spirited engagement watched by all Charles Town ensued. When the *Eagle*, flying the Jolly Roger, tried to flee, the men of Charles Town captured her, only to find she contained convicts and indentured servants (including thirty-six women). The pirates had earlier captured the vessel bringing them from England to America. Its captain, Richard Worley, was killed during the engagement.

Bonnet, when recaptured, made a pious appeal for his life, and even Colonel Rhett was so moved that he offered to take him to London to plead for a pardon. However, justice triumphed and in the autumn of 1718 Stede Bonnet and twenty-nine others were hanged. Later, nineteen of the crew of Richard Worley's *Eagle* were hanged also; their bodies buried on White Point shoal, just above the low-water mark. Nothing is ever really lost or forgotten in Charleston and the spot has since been incorporated into White Point Gardens on the Battery. The stroller, as he passes the walls of St. Philip's churchyard, can see the grave of Colonel William Rhett (1666-1722) with the inscription on the stone: "Late of this parish Principall Officer of his Majesties Customs in this Province: a kind husband, a faithful friend, a charitable neighbour, a religious constant worshipper of God."

We know that in 1752 that a Spanish *guardacosta* with a French crew "seized a vessel bound from Jamaica to Charles Town off Mole St. Nicholas," and that Samuel Parkes and Benjamin Hawks were hanged for piracy as late as 1760. However, the hanging of Stede Bonnet and the others sounded the death knell of piracy.

Following the peace of the Yemassee War and Queen Anne's War, development was still restricted beyond the lines of the city's old walls. By 1720 visitors from England or from the northern coastal cities could only with difficulty find a few trading posts, hamlets and crossroad settlements more than thirty miles outside Charles Town. Although the city was a center of the southern fur trade, it did not in actuality serve a large area. There was, by that time, however, a developing inland trade. The primitive footpaths through the forest, trod by the solitary trapper, gave way to larger ones, then to roads which followed earlier Indian trails, and Charles Town's trade in frontier products flourished. We are told that after 1720 the foundations were laid for fortunes which were later invested in plantations by Jonathan Amory, Samuel Everleigh, Edward Laughton, Arthur Middleton, Madam Sarah Rhett and Samuel Wragg.

T HE long-simmering agitation between the citizens and the Proprietors finally came to a head in 1719. As early as 1706, the friction, there from the beginning, determined the colonists to send to London their representative Joseph Boone—one of many emissaries who sailed to Britain to present Charles Town's grievances before the government. The purpose of Boone's journey was to protest a bill making it necessary for all members of the Commons House to take an oath in support of the Church of England.

When the Proprietors failed to see the case from his and the colonists' viewpoint, Boone took it to the House of Lords. In so doing he employed Daniel Defoe, a Dissenter and the author of *Robinson Crusoe*, to prepare for the Dissenters in Charles Town a brief, which was upheld by the House of Lords.

This was but a prelude to the internecine warfare that developed between the two groups and led, finally, to the overthrow of the Proprietary government in 1719. The populace, which had suppressed an Indian uprising—the Yemassee War—and curtailed piracy, informed the Governor by letter that it was determined to take over the Government. Not even two British warships in the harbor could dissuade them.

The insurrection was a harbinger of others—that in 1775, the Nullification crisis of 1832, and the Civil War in 1861.

WITH Europe at peace, more or less, from 1713 until 1743, the colonies enjoyed the same respite and period of relative calm. Charles Town, as did the other colonial cities, came of age socially, culturally, politically and economically. By the latter date two generations of Charlestonians had grown to majority from the time of the birth of Robert Tradd, the first white male child born in the city about 1679 to Richard and Elizabeth Tradd.

"Early in the century," Carl Bridenbaugh tells us, "the city became the center from which the richest planters ruled the province—a city state in which the state ruled the city. As the capital grew into a large community and faced the usual urban situations, its inhabitants deplored the absence of an independent and rationalized local administration. Prior to 1712 the Assembly governed the town directly by designating commissioners drawn from the Commons House to supervise the execution of each act pertaining to Charles Town."

The St. Andrew's Society was formed in 1729 and less than ten years later the South Carolina Society, which met Tuesdays at Poinsett's Tavern and brought together the wealthiest and most prominent citizens. Taverns were popular gathering places in the eighteenth century, and meetings were held in them in the absence of large public halls. The St. George's Society met and held its suppers at Robert Raper's Tavern. All these organizations were instrumental in helping the city's poor.

The Huguenot contribution to Charles Town was an important one, and none contributed more so than Lewis Timothy. Originally Louis Timothée, he was the son of a French Protestant who had taken refuge in Holland at the revocation of the Edict of Nantes. Timothée arrived in

South Carolina Society Hall, 72 Meeting Street, 1804-1825. Designed by Gabriel Manigault, a member of the Society, the first floor was used as a charity school, and the hall on the second floor—embellished by Adam decoration—was for the Society's meetings. Added later (1825), the portico was so designed by Frederick Wesner that it seems to be an integral part of the building itself. Frances B. Johnston photograph, *circa* 1930. Library of Congress.

CHARLESTOWN,
South-Carolina.

WHEREAS in and by An Act of the GENERAL ASSEMBLY of this Province, passed the 20th Day of *August*, 1731. "It is ENACTED, " That all Persons residing within the Province of *South-Carolina*, who in their " own Right, as likewise all Guardians, Executors, Trustees and Attorneys, who " in Right of others, do hold or claim any Messuages, Lands, Tenements or Hereditaments, " within the said Province, by virtue of any Patents or Grants from the late Lords Proprie- " tors, or their Governors, Deputies, Commissioners or Trustees, or by virtue of any Mesne " Conveyances under such original Patentees or Grantees, shall within eighteen Months after " the passing of the said Act, register all and every such their Patents, Grants, Mesne Con- " veyances, Deeds or Wills respectively, or Memorials thereof, in the Office of his Majesty's " Auditor General of this Province, or his Deputy, except Grants of Lots within the Town- " plats of Townships already laid out, and Leashold Estates only. And also that all Mort- " gagees of Lands and Tenements in this Province, having any such original Grants or Mesne " Conveyances, &c. in their Hands, of the Mortgageors, shall register the same or a Memo- " rial thereof in manner aforesaid. AND FURTHER, that in case such Persons, " who shall have registred their Lands, &c. as aforesaid, shall afterwards sell or dispose of " the same, or any part thereof, they shall cause a new Memorial to be made of the In- " denture or Deed, by which the same are conveyed, to be exhibited and filed with His " Majesty's Auditor General, or his Deputy: And, if devised by Will, then the Devisee, Ex- " ecutors, or Administrators shall exhibit a Memorial of such Will to be filed as aforesaid.

"AND IT IS FURTHER ENACTED, BY THE AUTHORITY " aforesaid, That all Lands whatsoever lying and being within the said Province of *South- Carolina*, now in the Tenure or Occupation of any Person or Persons whatsoever living and " residing within the same Province, that shall not be registred in the Office of the said " Auditor General, or his Deputy, within eighteen Months after the said Office shall be e- " rected, and established in *Charlestown*, and publick Notice given thereof by the said Audi- " tor General, or his Deputy, the same shall be reputed, deemed, and taken as vacant " Lands; and it shall be lawful for any Person to take up the same.

THIS is therefore to give Notice, that *James St. John*, Esq; being appointed by His Majesty, Auditor General of this Province, hath now opened his Office in *Charlestown*, in order to register all such Grants, Patents, Mesne Conveyances, Deeds, Wills, &c. or Me- morials thereof, to be filed as aforesaid, as shall be brought to him the said Auditor General, or his Deputy, for that Purpose. And that Attendance will be given at the Office of the said Auditor General, every Day, from the Hours of Nine to Twelve in the Forenoon, and from Two to Five in the Afternoon, Sundays and Holidays excepted.

Signed by Order of His Majesty's said Auditor General, this 27th Day of November, 1731.

Daniel Gibson dep Auditor

CHARLESTOWN: Printed by *T. Whitmarsh* at the Sign of the Table-Clock on the Bay, where all Sorts of Printing is performed at reasonable Rates.

Broadside. Imprint of the first year of printing in the colony from the only known copy in the Public Records Office, London. U. S. Bureau of Public Records.

Philadelphia in 1731 with his wife and four children, and in the following year had established a connection in an editorial capacity with Benjamin Franklin's short-lived *Philadelphische Zeitung,* the first German-language newspaper in America.

In 1733 we find him working for Franklin as a journeyman-printer. On November 26 of that year, a partnership agreement between the two was effected whereby Timothée would conduct a printing business in Charles Town as successor to Thomas Whitmarsh, Franklin's former partner there, who died in September, 1733.

On February 2, 1734, Timothée revived the *South-Carolina Gazette*, which had ceased publication on Whitmarsh's death, and in the following April Timothée anglicized the spelling of his name.

Until his death in 1738, Timothy continued as printer and publisher of the newspaper, and was the printer of the most ambitious and important production of the colonial press in South Carolina—*The Laws of the Province of South-Carolina* (1736), compiled by Nicholas Trott. He also printed legislative acts, tracts on the smallpox, essays on currency and *A Collection of Psalms and Hymns* (1737), the earliest Wesley collection in America.

In his *Autobiography*, Franklin said of Timothy and his wife: "He was a man of learning, and honest but ignorant in matters of account; and, tho' he sometimes made me remittances, I could get no account from him, nor any satisfactory state of our partnership while he lived. On his decease the business was continued by his widow, who being born and bred in Holland, where, as I have been inform'd, the knowledge of accounts makes a part of female education, she not only sent me as clear a statement as she could find of the transactions past, but continued to account with the greatest regularity and exactness every quarter afterwards, and managed the business with such success that she not only brought up reputedly a family of children, but, at the expiration of the term, was able to purchase of me the printing-house and establish her son [Peter] in it."

IN 1737 or 1738, the family of George Lucas sailed from the island of Antigua, their destination Charles Town. Not only was it to be their final port of call, but one of the daughters, Eliza, was to carve out her unique destiny in Charles Town and the countryside beyond. Born in 1723, Eliza was a young woman still in her teens when she came to live in St. Andrew's Parish on Wappoo Creek. In about 1740 she wrote: "Charles Town. . .is a quiet agreeable place, the people live very Gentile and very much in the English taste."

When her father returned to his interests in Antigua (he was lieutenant governor), she remained in charge of his plantation, her invalid mother, two brothers and a sister. From her letters to him, and others, we have a vivid picture of life on the plantation and in town. Rice, the great staple crop, could only be grown "where inland swamps could be conveniently watered from a banked 'reserve," and was the sole agricultural commodity.

By 1742 Eliza, convinced that indigo could be profitably grown in Carolina, wrote to her father that she must have seed by March in order to harvest it before frost settled in. That year "the price [of rice] is so low as thirty shillings pr. hundred, we have sent very little to town yet, for that reason." (The Winyah Indigo Society was founded in 1753 by plantation owners. Initiation fees and dues were paid in indigo and profits from its sale educated orphans.)

On November 11 of that year Eliza spoke of King George II's birthnight ball, and reported the controversy between the Reverend Commissary Garden and the Reverend George Whitfield. Garden was charged to "watch not only over the morals of the clergy, but to enforce their observance of the rules and forms prescribed by the church." When Whitfield, the fiery orator, was summoned before an ecclesiastical court, his advocate was Andrew Rutledge.

Eliza, later to marry Colonel Charles Pinckney and become the mother of both Thomas and Charles Cotesworth Pinckney, often rose at five o'clock in the morning to attend to her full schedule of running the plantation, teaching the Negro children to read and write, and to read voluminously herself in French and English. Her enduring contribution to Charleston's history, other than her ideal, was the successful cultivation of indigo, which gave the small colony an entirely new and marketable commodity.

Thomas Rose House, 59 Church Street, circa 1735. *Built four square on an asymmetrical plan with a high-pitched, hipped roof. The original entrance was through a door now replaced by a window on the extreme right; the street entrance and piazzas are modern additions.* Robert W. Tebbs photograph, Library of Congress.

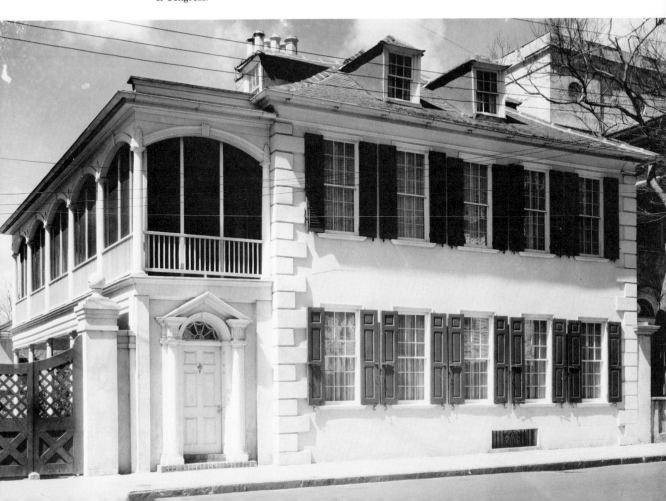

The Pinckney Mansion, where Eliza Lucas Pinckney lived, dated from about 1745 and commanded a sweeping view of the Cooper River. It was one of the casualties of the Civil War. Mathew Brady Collection. U.S. War Department General Staff photograph in the National Archives.

Charles Cotesworth Pinckney (1746-1825). A son of Charles and Eliza Lucas Pinckney, and a general in his own right during the Revolution, he was— with his cousin Charles—a delegate to the Constitutional Convention in Philadelphia in 1787. A special envoy to France in the years 1796 and 1797, he was an unsuccessful Federalist candidate for vice-president in 1800, and for president in 1804 and 1808. Pastel by James Sharples in the Independence National Historical Park Collection. Library of Congress.

Her diaries, letterbooks and the surviving letters themselves provide a vivid picture of life in the colony over two centuries ago. To her brother George, in England for his education, she wrote (*circa* 1741-1743):

> *Crs. Town the metropolis is a neat pretty place. The inhabitants polite and live in a very gentile manner. The streets and houses regularly built—the ladies and gentle men gay in their dress, upon the whole you will find as many agreeable people of both sexes for the size of the place*

as almost any where. St. Phillip's church in Crs. Town is a very elegant one, and much frequented. There are several more places of public worship in this town, and the generality of people of a religious turn of mind—

This observation was borne out by John Lawson, an English government surveyor, who wrote: "This colony was first planted by a genteel sort of people that were well acquainted with the trade, and had either money or parts to make good use of the advantages that offered, as most have done by raising themselves to great estates. . . ."

Eliza's great friend was the wife of Colonel Pinckney, and when the first Mrs. Pinckney died, the childless soldier married Eliza. Her range of interests was amazing, especially so for a young woman of her years, her time, and with the little formal education she had. The appearance of comets, the condition of the crops, politics and the balls which were part of Charles Town life, nature—"but I own I love the vegitable world extreamly," the amusements of town and country all fascinated Eliza. An advanced young woman, although she would have been the last to think so, she drew up wills for people in her district and firmly stood up to her father on the matter of an arranged marriage.

Eliza, whose portrait has not survived, left two enduring legacies to her adopted South Carolina. Indigo, until after the Revolution when the British bounties were dropped, gave the colony an exportable crop in addition to rice. And Eliza's sons and descendants contributed as richly in their ways as she had to Charleston's and South Carolina's history. Thomas was Minister to the Court of St. James's and to Spain, and Charles Cotesworth Pinckney was involved in the XYZ affair in 1797. It was he who said: "Millions for defence, but not one cent for tribute."

Eliza died in 1793 in Philadelphia, having gone there in search of medical treatment. She lies in an unmarked grave in St. Peter's Churchyard, which seems ironic since President Washington attended her funeral. A small memorial stone was placed in the churchyard in recent years. For some unexplained reason Charleston has failed to erect a monument to her memory, but her spirit hovers over the city and today she is spoken of by many as an old friend, or a spiritual forbear.

CHARLES TOWN, the focal point of the life of the Low Country gentry, began to take on the mellowness of age even though a fire in 1740 destroyed nearly all the seventeenth-century buildings and reconstruction—one of many, past and

Detail in the garden wall of the Colonel John Stuart House. Marjorie R. Maurer photograph.

The Joseph Manigault House, Meeting Street and Ashmead Place, circa *1790. Detail of bay photographed about 1930, showing the lovely old brick. The architect for the house was Gabriel Manigault (1758-1809), who designed it for his brother. It has been described as being "the first dwelling house to be planned* de nouveau *to suit the requirements of the owner instead of following the often repeated plans of either the single or the double house."*
Frances B. Johnston photograph. Library of Congress.

to come—had to be undertaken. St. Philip's survived the fire but regulations that required buildings to be of stone or brick and forbade the erection of new wharves were now relaxed or ignored. However, there were to be no wooden shingles after December 20, 1745. In a ten-year period one hundred lots alone contained eighty-four new structures. Among these were ones for fifty merchants and some artisans, several of which were handsome indeed, such as those of Captain Henry Frankland and Chief Justice Benjamin Whitaker. There was a tavern, a dram shop, and even an establishment for a dancing master! Two Philadelphia Quakers, William Logan and James Pemberton, reported in 1745 that the gentry "live in the Genteelest manner and are Exceedingly civil and kind to strangers."

No sooner had Charles Town figuratively gotten on its feet again than it faced disaster once more. On September 15, 1752, the "most destructive hurricane ever known" struck about 9:00 A.M. and in two hours had "reduced this Town to a very melancholy situation." Vessels were driven ashore and wharves in turn were washed away. "Nothing was now to be seen but ruins of houses, canows, wrecks of pettiauguas and boats, masts, yards, incredible quantities of all sorts of timber, barrels, staves, shingles, household and other goods, floating and driving, with great violence thro' the streets, and round about the Town."

On White Point alone—always a most vulnerable situation—out of two hundred dwellings, few could be seen still standing. In all some five hundred houses were demolished and a fortnight later, before the debris could be cleared away, another great wind came, frightening the citizenry but otherwise doing little damage. Because of these natural catastrophes, Charles Town in 1760 gave an impression of newness, so much so that *The American Gazetteer* reported the houses were "large, some of brick, but more of timber and generally sashed, and let at excessive rates." The skyline as seen from the harbor was impressive and some of the city's buildings rivaled those of the mother country.

For over two hundred years the Castor and Pollux of

Charles Town have been the spires and facades of St. Philip's and St. Michael's. It would be difficult to conceive of the city without either or both. St. Michael's did not come into being until the parish of St. Philip's was divided. Begun in 1752, St. Michael's was not opened for services until 1761. Its construction was followed by a spate of building. Opposite St. Michael's another State House and a new market house began to take shape in 1753, and to give this intersection of Broad and Meeting Streets the beginning of the elegance it has since retained. The State House, gone these many years, was described by Dr. James Milligan as "a large commodious Brick Building. . .decorated with 2/3 Columns of the Composite Order, whose Capitals are highly finished, supporting a large angular Pediment and Cornice. . . ."

In May of 1752 Dr. John Lining in Charles Town repeated Benjamin Franklin's kite experiment only to have the wrath of the Fundamentalists descend on him because of his "meddling with Heaven's Artillery." This fear of lightning drove the South Carolina Assembly to order lightning rods for the Powder Magazine and Fort Johnson. Dr. Lining is remembered, too, for the accurate description he wrote of the yellow fever epidemic of 1748. It was published first in 1753 by Peter Timothy and later that year in the *Edinburgh Medical Journal*.

Interior detail in St. Michael's.
Marjorie R. Maurer photograph.

Charleston is ironwork, old brick and St. Philip's.
Marjorie R. Maurer photograph.

St. Michael's watches over Charleston, as does St. Philip's. Here the steeple of St. Michael's is seen in all its elegance and simplicity from the entry garden of the Russell House. Marjorie R. Maurer photograph.

TODAY the streets of Charleston are immaculate, tidy, well swept. In 1758 the Commons House of South Carolina voted £ 550 for the improvement of the town's streets. Earlier in 1744 the Grand Jury had requested a public scavenger—a term then current for a crossing sweeper—but it was not until 1750 that there was appointed a man of all utility, who would see to cleaning, filling up or repairing all streets, drains or sewers. After 1755 citizens were fined twenty shillings if they "fouled a way after it had been cleaned."

The situation was dire enough for Peter Timothy to print in the *South-Carolina Gazette* an article entitled "The Remonstrance of the Streets of Charles Town against the Inhabitants." The streets, humanized in the piece, admonished Charlestonians because they allowed "a Number of little, narrow, dirty and irregular Alleys and Lanes" to be opened for private use, leaving them "dirty, poluting the air, and a disgrace to the capital of a great and flourishing province." Negroes were forbidden to ride horses within the city and sedan chairs, a commonplace sight, often caused traffic problems—especially on Sundays at St. Philip's.

Charles Town's growing importance was seen in every facet of the city's life. The annual rice fleet was a familiar sight (because Charles Town had no fleet itself, the other coastal cities shared in the re-exportation of the rice and indigo crops), and the harbor was filled with vessels of every shape and kind from either the northern ports or those of the Caribbean. Charles Town was in a unique position—the last port of importance on the Atlantic Coast, in a way a jumping-off place between the mainland colonies and those European ones in the West Indies.

Into this peaceful growing period—when Charles Town was entering into its own as a fair-sized city—intruded the distant sounds of war. In North America it was first King

Dogs must wait outside St. Philip's.   Marjorie R. Maurer photograph.

George's War (1744-1748), known in Europe as the War of the Austrian Succession. The French and Indian War (1754-1760) was a prelude and, for the colonists, a training ground for the Revolution.

With war came certain new regulations and restrictions—the British acts of trade and navigation, which limited trade among the colonies, mother country, and the rest of the world. Charles Town's—and Carolina's—chief crops were rice and Eliza Lucas Pinckney's indigo, but large quantities of foodstuffs and other goods were imported. Flour and bread, from Philadelphia, for instance, were exchanged for such items as rice, turpentine, leather, potatoes and oranges.

Cheese, butter, even rum and beer, were imported from the northern cities and wines from Spain and Portugal. Inexpensive furniture came from Newport, sea coal from Nova Scotia, and slaves were now brought from the Guinea coast of Africa to be sold at the slave mart. In addition to the exchange of actual goods, Charlestonians were often to be found traveling by sea up the coast to Philadelphia, New York, Newport and Boston. Benjamin Franklin at one point supplied Peter Timothy with paper for the *South-Carolina Gazette*.

Although strung along the coast like so many jewels on a chain necklace, these colonial cities were continually in con-

Charleston, circa 1860. Drawn by J.W. Hill. Engraved by Weltwood & Peters.   Print and Picture Department, Free Library of Philadelphia.

tact, despite their separation by distance. Charles Town and Savannah were in constant communication: ships plied between them regularly. Charles Town remained capital of the colony as well as the titular capital of the region from St. Simon's Island and parts of Georgia on the south to the Pee Dee River of the north.

The French and Indian War, with the constant fear of attacks and reprisals by the French and Spanish, prevented the hinterlands being developed to their full potential. But once the expansion began it opened up new possibilities for Carolinians, and importations from Philadelphia and other northern cities were reduced. Rice, indigo and later cotton were the chief exports to England, but until the middle of the eighteenth century dressed deerskins accounted for sixteen

percent of the city's exports to Britain. South Carolina's coastal highways—the rivers that webbed the coastline and snaked inland—brought these products to the port of Charles Town.

Piracy as such was dying, but another more gentlemanly pursuit, privateering, was practiced. Northern privateers were outfitted in Charles Town, letters of marque issued, and there was a certain activity in the prize courts of the town as well. It is worthwhile noting that during the French and Indian War that Charles Town was "the only city not deeply committed to trade with the enemy."

New England supplied new ships; Charles Town's shipbuilding having faltered during King George's War. Arts and crafts in Charles Town, especially after 1750, did not flourish—although there were fine silversmiths and furniture makers—as they did in other colonies. This was in part due to the lack of shipbuilding. However, a successful craftsman often left his trade, invested his money in land and slaves, and became a planter. After all, the real aristocracy of South Carolina consisted chiefly of the plantation owners, those whose fortunes depended on rice and indigo, and every tradesman aspiring to ascend the social ladder knew this. Henry Laurens is an excellent illustration of this. Son of a saddler, he was an example of the self-made man, rising from artisan to a position in a counting house. Much of Laurens' trade was with Moravians of Bethabara and Salem, North Carolina, three hundred miles northward.

Henry Laurens (1724-1792). Extraordinarily successful as a merchant and a planter, nothing but ill-fortune stalked Laurens the statesman. Politically a moderate, his sensitivity to criticism caused him to resign from the presidency of the Second Continental Congress (1777-1778). Captured off Newfoundland en route to negotiate a treaty with the Dutch, he was imprisoned in the Tower of London (1780-1781), to be released only after signing damaging claims of loyalty. He assisted with negotiations for peace in Paris, but there ended his public career. Portrait by Charles Willson Peale, 1784. Independence National Historical Park Collection.

An apprentice system did exist and often these trainees were orphans or illegitimate children without homes, who were charges of the parish. Indentured servants were commonplace—Charles Town being one of their chief ports of entry (Philadelphia was another)—but rather than being apprenticed they were usually indentured to landowners beyond the borders of the city.

It is noteworthy too that only in Charles Town did Negro artisans pose serious competition for white craftsmen. They were permitted by their owners to daily stand for hire, or were rented out for specific times. One of their specialties was the calking or mending of boats. This practice, little remembered today, was widespread enough to cause one citizen, Andrew Ruck, in 1744 to petition the Commons House on behalf of the shipwrights.

Wages went to the slave owner, providing him with another source of revenue from his investment, and endangered the white freeman's livelihood. By 1751 the practice was widespread enough to cause concern, and slaves (unless they were owned by orphans!) were forbidden by the authorities to hire out as porters, laborers or fisherman.

Names prominent in Charles Town's history are recorded as merchants. Gabriel Manigault was a wholesaler; another, Christopher Gadsden, profited by the war by dealing in belts, lace for hats and carbines; and J. P. Grimké and Joshua Lockwood dealt in jewelry. These men of commerce often outfitted peddlers with pack horses, sending them into the back country and the interior. The war itself forced Charles Town to import corn from Virginia and from the northern colonies.

Christopher Gadsden (1724-1805). Early on he established himself as a Revolutionary radical. A delegate to the Stamp Act Congress in 1765, he was among those who argued for the union of the colonies against the authority of Parliament. More of a prosperous merchant and ideologist than a soldier, Gadsden nevertheless left the Continental Congress to take command of South Carolina's forces. Always in the thick of political controversy, he was, nonetheless, a conspicuous member of the Assembly of South Carolina for nearly thirty years. Independence National Historical Park Collection.

Gate House of the Manigault House. The design here was influenced by Italian classic forms, and Manigault himself was most likely influenced by Robert Adam, who was "the first architect using the classic vocabulary of Roman antiquity to make the distinction between the scale of classic temples and other public buildings and the smaller scale appropriate for domestic architecture." Frances B. Johnston photograph, *circa* 1930. Library of Congress.

PEACE came in welcome, but sporadic, periods in the eighteenth century, whose history was fraught with wars. It came once more in 1760, although hostilities continued in the Caribbean. England captured Havana and Martinique, molasses and sugar stopped arriving from the West Indies, and rice exports in 1761-1762 dropped a third in Charles Town. The colonies felt the change from war to peace. With the coming of peace, Charles Town, no longer a town, achieved the status of a city. It was, and would be for some time to come, a city-state. To many in the city the wars had brought prosperity. Others were ruined by business losses. The year also saw a new king—George III—on the throne, and many Charlestonians purchased mourning when learning of the death of his grandfather, George II.

The excesses of the eighteenth century were evident in Charles Town, although naturally on a smaller scale. Peace might exist between England, France and Spain, but there were racial tensions. St. Philip's parish instituted a mounted patrol to apprehend all blacks out without passes, or not accompanied by their masters. During the war there were highway robberies by soldiers and sailors—those sources of constant mischief—but Charles Town did escape the large incidence of crime which occurred in other cities.

Because it was a port, and the only city of consequence in the southern colonies, it had its share of paupers—most of them immigrants who arrived penniless. The vestry of St. Philip's—always cognizant of the city's needs—assumed responsibility for the immigrants, mariners without means, and wives and children of soldiers. Some Acadians from Nova Scotia found their way to Charles Town and in 1757 the vestry alloted three hundred pounds for clothes for these unfortunate wanderers. It also added to the workhouse room for indigents and a building for the insane, and paid Dr. Alexander Garden and Dr. George Milligan for calling on the sick.

Other than Philadelphia, which suffered from regular and devastating epidemics in the eighteenth century, Charles Town more than other cities seemed to be plagued with these. Yellow fever and diphtheria were common, and the pesthouse—that horror of the time—was isolated on Sullivan's Island. Worst of all was the smallpox, a scourge of the eighteenth century, which was carried to the city in 1760 by Cherokee Indians.

Charles Town was in a state of panic. The *South-Carolina Gazette* carried an article on inoculation by Dr. William Heberden of London, which Benjamin Franklin had earlier circulated in most of the colonial cities. In a fortnight between twenty-four hundred and twenty-eight hundred were inoculated. With the fear of the disease there was the added problem of declining stores. The panic spread to the country people who feared the pestilence to such a degree that they hesitated to bring food into the city. The plague, beginning February 2, continued until July before abating, and many merchants did not return until December. About three hundred whites and three hundred and fifty Negroes died of it. There was one comforting note to the entire terrible year: most citizens contracted the pox in some form, and as a result of their immunity were spared infection for what remained of the colonial period.

By 1760 the population reached eight thousand from sixty-eight hundred in 1743, not as great an increase as in the northern cities, but certainly an evidence of growth. There was a mellowness upon the city itself that only age could give it. Long before the term reconstruction was applied to the era following the Civil War, Charles Town had adopted it as its watchword. If it wasn't reconstruction following fire that con-

Miles Brewton House, 27 King Street, circa *1767. One of the most important houses in Charleston it has been called the supreme example of the double house in the city. Because of its spaciousness and sumptuous interior, the house during the British occupation became the headquarters of Sir Henry Clinton, Lord Rawdon and the Marquess Cornwallis. In 1865 it was occupied by Generals George Gordon Meade and John P. Hatch. It has been the home of some of Charleston's most distinguished families–Brewton, Motte, Alston, Pringle, Frost and Manigault–and has never passed out of the hands of the descendants of Miles Brewton, its builder.* Marjorie R. Maurer photograph.

cerned Charlestonians, it was reconstruction following hurricanes.

Fine old town houses appeared after 1750. Charles Town had not earlier thought of grand town houses, as we see them today. What were built were ones on a more modest scale than in London. Before this date planters had not remained long enough in town to warrant anything more elaborate. It was at this time of rebuilding that the Eveleigh House at 39 Church Street, the Huger House on Meeting Street, and Captain Thomas Franklin's residence date.

Charleston's Exchange Building, circa 1767-1772, survived the fire and the war. The shop at the corner, pictured here in 1865, in front of which the loungers are standing, was early on the Harris Tavern, later the French Coffee Shop. Now, true to its heritage, it is a private purveyor of wines and liquors. U.S. War Department General Staff photograph in the National Archives.

Social life advanced and was part of this new maturity, this patina of age. There were the Queen Street Theatre for theatrical productions and Mrs. Gordon's "Long Room" for balls. Lewis Hallam, already well-known in northern cities, brought the first professionally acted plays since 1736, when his company played from October to December, 1754. The subscription Assembly met at Blythe's Tavern in 1746 and by 1759 Charlestonians in increasing numbers were spending the summer at Newport. Joseph Durfree, who had a profitable trade in cordials, ciders, rum, codfish, potatoes, cheese, candles and whale oil at Beale's Wharf, on his scheduled trips to Charles Town "was master of the sloop *Charlestown*, in which he transported a number of South Carolinians and West Indians to Newport."

There was the York Course, a mile outside the city, the Newmarket Track at Goose Creek, and in 1754 Thomas Nightingale's "Charlestown Races." And the Carolina Jockey Club must not be forgotten. Charles Town in the eighteenth and nineteenth centuries was mad about racing.

IN this era of peace, cultural and commercial relations with Europe improved and advanced and, in the remaining sixteen years of the colonial period until the Declaration of Independence ended it forever, the population rose from eight thousand in 1760 to twelve thousand in 1776. Peace and the prospect of a new reign under a young monarch brought a sense of hope and contentment to Charles Town's citizens.

The inevitable hurricane, this time May 4, 1761, did its usual damage, and piers and shipping were destroyed. The estimates of the losses amounted to twenty thousand pounds. Christopher Gadsden persuaded the merchants to offset the destruction and, for the first time, wharves were constructed out into the Ashley River. Gadsden himself in 1767 began a "far more extensive operation than any colonial merchant had yet attempted when he framed a very long wharf that extended 840 feet into the water, with space for ten or twelve ships at a time." Samuel Prioleau, Jr., John Gaillard, William Gibbes, Captain Edward Black and Robert Mackenzie all followed his example and had wharves built. A storm in 1770 did considerable damage to these and others.

In 1761 Benjamin Smith could report to Ezra Stiles in Newport that there were only about four hundred houses in Charles Town, but when the colonial period finally closed there were approximately fifteen hundred of wood or brick. "Many of them have a genteel appearance, though generally incumbered with Balconies or Piazzas. . . ." Six street lamps appeared in 1762 and by 1770 twenty were placed "at the Public Expence," and one hundred more soon appeared as citizens hung them before their houses. A recession was felt in 1762 and taxes were higher, levied for payment of war debts.

In the five-year period after 1767, three hundred new houses were constructed, and the desolated area of White Point again became a showplace with mansions the plantation gentry maintained there for the summer season.

After 1764 a few brick six-foot-wide sidewalks appeared (there were no paved streets before this time). The condition of the streets was improved by turkey buzzards who consumed "what sloth has not removed out of the way, and so have a great part in maintaining cleanliness and keeping off unwholesome vapors from dead beasts and filth." Goats and swine were also scavengers.

A centenary enables citizens and historians alike to take a long backward glance, to judge the accomplishments, the progress and the growth of a city. By 1770 Charles Town had achieved a patina of age in spite of the constant rebuilding that storms, hurricanes and fires necessitated. The mansions along its broad, tree-lined streets bespoke prosperity;

*The central market, 1907. The buzzards, often called "Charleston Eagles,"
were the scavengers who kept the streets around the market clean.* Detroit
Publishing Company photograph. Library of Congress.

their contents were indications of the craftsman's art: fine
furniture, elegant silver, the costliest china. Portraits,
bibelots and *objets d'art* brought from visits to the northern
cities or to Europe filled the rooms of the elegant residences
alongside furniture by Charles Town's Thomas Elfe and silver
by Daniel You. The gardens were—as they have always
been—the horticulturist's art brought to its finest degree.

And, withal, there was a leisurely, patterned, organized
and structured way of life, which was outwardly controlled by
manners, customs, fashion and a great sense of gentility.
Charles Town, too, achieved a sense of independence. Its de-

Colonel John Stuart House, 106 Tradd Street, circa 1772. *A native of Scotland, Colonel Stuart came to Charleston about thirty years before the Revolution. The lookout at the ridge of the roof was used to observe ships entering the harbor or to witness the approach of an Indian chief down the path that is now King Street, for Colonel Stuart was for a time before the Revolution the superintendent of Indian Affairs.* Marjorie R. Maurer photograph.

pendence on England had lessened; the Proprietors were ghosts of the past. There was renewed vigor, the expectancy of entering a new age. Governor William Bull reported that in the centenary year "as many as three thousand wagons per year" arrived in town and in December, 1771, there were counted 113 teams on their way into the city. Flaxseed, flour and tobacco were staples that reached Charles Town by wagon from the inland communities.

This climate of commercial activity accelerated when in 1771 the Society for Encouraging Manufacturers established a subscription to stimulate trade. The relaxation of the pressure on colonial trade, with the repeal of the Stamp Act and the Townshend duties, proved to be a stimulus to many local industries, which increased in strength with the agitation about non-importation.

Several years later, in 1773, Josiah Quincy noted in his diary: "I can only say, in general, that in grandeur, splendour of buildings, decorations, equipages, numbers, commerce, shipping, and indeed in almost every thing, it [Charles Town] far surpasses all I ever saw, or ever expected to see, in America."

Colonel John Stuart House. Many of the interiors of the house were lost to museums elsewhere during the years following World War I, but a later owner, John Mead Howells, a distinguished architect, replaced much of the word carving in the drawing room. Marjorie R. Maurer photograph.

IF anything precipitated the American Revolution, it was the Stamp Act but, of course, there were other factors, too. The Stamp Act perforce meant that Americans could not buy and sell property, involve themselves in or collect debts, marry, execute wills or engage in commerce without paying a sum for a stamp which entitled them to do so. It inspired thoughts of liberty in American breasts.

In Charles Town some citizens opposed controversy with Great Britain, fearing it would endanger commerce between the two. Others felt concerted action was the only course which would enable Britain to see its error and make Parliament equally anxious that South Carolina remain a Royal Province. And there were those who wanted independence, notably Christopher Gadsden and William Johnson. The General Assembly opposed such an idea and John Rutledge, Thomas Lynch and Gadsden were sent to New York as delegates to the Stamp Act Congress, which convened there in October, 1765. In America Gadsden wanted independence, and in London William Pitt voted for repeal.

Civic pride was such that Charles Town had the honor of erecting the first statue in a public park in the colonies. The city honored this man with the voice of moderation who was its friend in Parliament. The South Carolina Assembly in 1766 appropriated seven thousand pounds for a likeness of William Pitt, first earl of Chatham (1708-1778), the great friend of provincial America who urged conciliation with the colonies. When the Royal Governor, thinking the expense unwarranted, refused to sign the bill, the planters defied him—the spirit of revolt was in the air—and took matters into their hands.

The sculpture, classical in the tradition of the day, was executed by Joseph Wilton, sculptor of the memorial to General James Wolfe in Westminster Abbey. It was set up in the center of Broad and Meeting Streets and remained there in

The statue of William Pitt, first Earl of Chatham, by Joseph Wilton stands in
Washington Park today. It was erected against much opposition and protest
and lost an arm during the British shelling of Charles Town during the
Revolution. It is as affectionately thought of in Charleston as are the spires of
St. Michael's and St. Philip's. Marjorie R. Maurer photograph.

John Rutledge (1739-1800). A member of the Stamp Act Congress of 1765, and of the Continental Congress (1774-1775; 1782-1783), he was also president of South Carolina from 1776 to 1778, and a signer of the Constitution. Before his death in Charleston he was chief justice of the state (1791-1795). Engraved from a drawing after the painting by John Trumbull. Library of Congress.

splendor until in 1780 it lost an arm from a British shell, fired from a battery on James Island.

Matters worsened in Charles Town, as they did elsewhere in the colonies. Tea was seized for non-payment of duty and stored in the Custom House by the Collector of Customs. Two years after the imposition of the Stamp Act, Charles Town, as did other coastal cities, learned that the Townshend

Acts imposed customs duties on imports of glass, lead, paints, paper, and tea. The result was the signing of non-importation agreements by the citizens of Charles Town.

Charlestonians, much like other colonials, had a new sense of independence after the long years of the French and Indian War, but although the lamp of liberty shone dimly then, it increased in intensity in proportion to the acts of agression by King George's government. Charles Town, and for that matter, the Low Country generally, had a sense of affinity with Britain. Customs, manners, architecture and the education of its sons were British. The leisurely, mannered life in Charles Town had much in common with that of the gentry in Britain. At first there was no thought of a rupture between the two.

Events moved slowly, though in retrospect they seem to have gone quickly. A Convention was called in July, 1774, to protest the Boston Port Bill, when Parliament closed that harbor after the "tea party." The *South-Carolina Gazette* called it "the largest body of the most respectable inhabitants ever seen together in Charles Town." This was followed by the First Continental Congress, when Henry Middleton, John Rutledge, Christopher Gadsden, Thomas Lynch and Edward Rutledge journeyed north to Philadelphia to participate in the events at Carpenters' Hall in September and October, 1774.

John Adams in his *Autobiography* reveals that the committee appointed to prepare a Declaration of Rights had reached an impasse on the question of Parliament's authority. Some committee members were "for a flat denial of all authority; others for denying the power of taxation only; some for denying internal, but admitting external taxation." When it seemed they would never agree, Adams says:

Mr. John Rutledge of South Carolina, one of the Committee, addressing himself to me, was pleased to say, "Adams, we must agree upon something; you appear to be as familiar with the subject as any of us, and I like your expres-

sions. . .and I am determined against all taxation for revenue. Come, take the pen and see if you can't produce something that will unite us."

The following January the Provincial Congress met in Charles Town and Charles Pinckney, its president, appointed a committee—William Henry Drayton was its chairman—to examine "the defenses of the province and the safety of the people." The same delegation which attended the First Continental Congress was present at the Second which met at the State House in Philadelphia on May 10, 1775.

Carolinians were isolated from other colonies, and from large centers of population in the north by distance and by lines of communication. The spirit of resistance was in the air, but settlers in the Up Country knew little of the issues that had now become sore points between the Low Country and Parliament.

On July 17, 1775, Lord William Campbell arrived as the new Royal Governor. Lord William had one point in his favor: he was married to the former Sarah Izard of Charles Town. Although Lord William and Lady Sarah were treated with courtesy, it was well known that the Izards had joined the ranks of the rebels. Events were accelerating. Christopher Gadsden and his friends met beneath the Liberty Tree, and William Drayton obtained twenty-two thousand pounds of powder, and sent five thousand pounds of it to George Washington. The countryside was astir with preparations; some factions were loyal to the King and many of their members deserted to the British side.

The second Provincial Congress met in Charles Town on November 1, 1775. By this time Tories were forced to leave the province, and Lord William Campbell was organizing the discontents. A large expedition against the city was expected in late 1775, and the Committee of Safety ordered Colonel William Moultrie to take possession of Fort Johnson.

The dawning of 1776 was in itself uneventful in Charles Town, but within weeks events were brought to a point of crisis. John Rutledge was elected president of South Carolina

Charles Pinckney (1757-1824). A member of Congress from South Carolina in 1785 and again from 1819 to 1821, he was a member of the Constitutional Convention of 1787 and one of the South Carolina signers of that document. He was subsequently governor of South Carolina from 1789 to 1792, from 1796 to 1798, and again from 1806 to 1808. A United States senator from 1798 to 1801, he was appointed United States minister to Spain (1802-1805) by Thomas Jefferson. Painted by Rembrandt Peale, circa *1795-1797.* Library of Congress.

on March 26. A provisional government was formed and, as well, a Council of Safety, which numbered thirteen. Henry Laurens was president of the latter, with Rawlins Lowndes, William Henry Drayton and Arthur Middleton among its members.

Everyone was involved in some manner of preparation for the promised assault on the city. Drayton and Thomas Heyward, Jr., sank four old boats loaded with stone in Hog

N.b[y] E. View of the Fort on the Western end of Sulivans Island with the Disposition of His Majesty's Fleet Commanded by Commodore Sir Peter Parker Kn. &c. &c. &c. during the Attack on the 28th of June 1776, which lasted 9 hours and 40 minutes. Presented by Lt. Colonel Thos. James, R. R. of Artillery, June 30th, 1776. London. Engrav'd and Publish'd according to Act of Parliament Aug. 10th 1776, by Wm. Faden Corner of St. Martins Lane Charing Cross. Courtesy, Museum of Early Southern Decorative Arts, Winston-Salem, N.C.

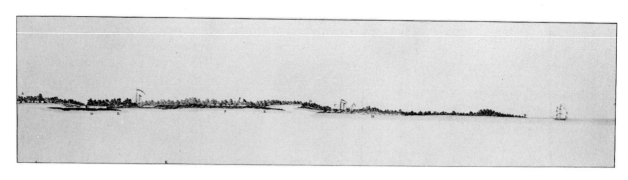

A Bird's Eye View from Part of Mount Pleasant . . . [to] The Fort on Sulivans Island by Lt. Colonel Thos. James, R. R. of Artillery, July 1, 1776. London. Engrav'd and Publish'd according to Act of Parliament Augt. 10, 1776, by Wm. Faden Corner of St. Martins Lane Charing Cross. Courtesy, Museum of Early Southern Decorative Arts, Winston-Salem, N.C.

Island Channel to the north of the shoal called Shute's Folly (later Castle Pinckney). A fort (afterwards Fort Moultrie) was erected on Sullivan's Island, which was fired on by the British ships *Tamar* and *Cherokee* when they tried to enter the harbor; and Gadsden, who favored forming a regular government, startled a meeting on February 1, 1776, by espousing Thomas Paine's *Common Sense,* only to be rebuked by John Rutledge. When the Congress and the citizens heard Parliament had declared the colonies in rebellion, and ordered property seized, reconciliation was a hope of the past.

Such rebellion and protest could only lead to the invasion long anticipated. A British fleet under the command of Sir Peter Parker, with two hundred and twenty guns and twenty-three hundred regulars (the troops were commanded by Sir Henry Clinton), was seen off the bar. Although the harbor channels were intricate, contained submerged sandbanks, and had to be sounded, the fleet managed to penetrate to a point between Fort Johnson on James Island and the hastily, but ingeniously, constructed fort on Sullivan's Island.

N.W. b[y] N. View of Charles Town . . . taken in Five Fathom Hole the day after the Attack upon Fort Sulivan by the Commodore & his Squadron which Action continued 9 hours & 40 minutes. London. Engrav'd and Publish'd according to Act of Parliament Augt. 10th 1776, by Wm. Faden Corner of St. Martins Lane Charing Cross. Courtesy, Museum of Early Southern Decorative Arts, Winston-Salem, N.C.

Confrontation came on June 28, 1776. The British bombarded the palmetto fort, even severing the pole holding the flag. In one of those acts of bravery that history remembers, Sergeant William Jasper raised the fallen flag after it was shot down. The British fleet suffered severe bombardment and withdrew. Casualties totaled 205 for the British and 37 for the Americans.

The result of this brave stand was that military operations against South Carolina were not renewed for over two and a half years, and the colony was allowed to remain in relative peace. While this period of peace reigned, trade with Britain ceased, the bounty on indigo was lost and all shipping was severely handicapped by the blockade.

IN Philadelphia events which affected the future of the colonies were witnessed by a number of South Carolinians. Four—Thomas Heyward, Jr., Thomas Lynch, Jr., Arthur Middleton and Edward Rutledge—were there to sign the Declaration of Independence. Heyward, a member of the Council of Safety and of the Second Continental Congress, had been admitted to the Middle Temple in 1765 and to the bar in South Carolina in 1771. Lynch was to die in his thirtieth year, when toward the close of 1779 he and his wife took passage aboard a vessel bound for the West Indies, and were never heard from again. Middleton also studied at the Middle Temple and was "one of the boldest members of the Council of Safety and its Secret Committee." Rutledge, governor of South Carolina, was a member of the Continental Congress from 1774 until 1776.

By January, 1778, the General Assembly convened and disestablished the Church of England as the official church. It also substituted for the legislative council elected from the General Assembly, a senate to be elected by the people of the election units. When the changes were adopted, John Rut-

Thomas Heyward, Jr. (1746-1809). Signer of the Declaration of Indepen-
dence, Heyward was the eldest son of Colonel Daniel Heyward, one of the
wealthiest planters in the colony, and of Mary Miles, daughter of William
Miles. Admitted to the Middle Temple, London, in 1765, and to the bar in
South Carolina in 1771, he was a delegate to the provincial convention which
met in Charleston on July 6, 1774, and a later one there on January 11, 1775.
He was one of the thirteen members of the Council of Safety, chosen by this
congress a few months later, which practically took over the functions of
government. Oil on canvas, copy by Charles Fraser, before 1851, after
Jeremiah Theus.   Independence National Historical Park Collection.

Edward Rutledge (1749-1800). Signer of the Declaration of Independence and brother of John Rutledge, he was a delegate to the first two Continental Congresses. It has been said that he was so uncertain about having signed the Declaration that he hesitated to tell his brother about it. Library of Congress.

ledge vetoed them and promptly resigned. A year later when the General Assembly (under the new constitution) met, Rutledge was elected governor (as the executive was then called) and served with distinction until January, 1782.

The British blockade began in 1776, but the *Randolph* managed to run it successfully and, in 1777, was able to return with four prizes. In January of the next year, when a fire leveled 250 houses in Charles Town, it was thought that the crew of one of the blockaders had infiltrated the city and set the blaze. This contest for supremacy of the sea was resolved somewhat when Alexander Gillon, commodore of the South Carolina navy, secured in Europe the frigate *South Carolina,* used it as a privateer and returned with many prizes. That year, too, the progress of the war was transferred to the Southern Department and Charles Town soon found that its interlude of peace was drawing to a close.

An initial attack upon the city in May, 1779, was led by General Augustine Prévost and when, on May 12, 1780, the city surrendered to Admiral Marriott Arbuthnot and Sir Henry Clinton, Charles Town's first occupation began. General Benjamin Lincoln and his troops were, unfortunately, a part of the capitulation. Lincoln wanted to evacuate his army, only to be opposed by Charles Cotesworth Pinckney and Christopher Gadsden. One fortuitous circumstance of the taking of Charles Town was the earlier escape of General (then Lieutenant Colonel) Francis Marion, the scion of an old Huguenot family. He had injured one leg jumping from a window to escape from an over-zealous Charleston host who had locked his doors, insisting his guests finish drinking! At the time of the city's capitulation Marion was at his home in St. John's Parish, Berkley.

Sir Henry Clinton on June 3, 1780, in a proclamation informed the citizens of Charles Town "that all inhabitants of the Province who are now prisoners on parole must take an active part in arms for the Royal Government or be treated as rebels." As Clinton was returning north and feeling that South Carolina was restored to the crown, he appealed for five thousand men. His request, rather than bringing in the required recruits, activated resistance in the form of guerilla warfare. Generals Andrew Pickens and Thomas Sumter led bands of men in the central and northern parts of the province against the British, and Francis Marion, the "Swamp Fox," and his marauders harrassed the enemy in the Low Country.

This now-legendary hero of the southern campaign was pictured by William Cullen Bryant in his "Song of Marion's Men":

> *Our band is few, but true and tried,*
> *Our leader frank and bold:*
> *The British soldier trembles*
> *When Marion's name is told.*
>
> *Our fortress is the good greenwood,*
> *Our tent the cypress-tree;*
> *We know the forest round us,*
> *As seamen know the sea.*
>
> *We know its walls of thorny vines,*
> *Its glades of reedy grass,*
> *Its safe and silent islands*
> *Within the dark morass.*

Thomas Sumter (1734-1832). A veteran of Indian warfare, Sumter's fierceness and intrepidy earned for him the soubriquet "Carolina Gamecock," or "Gamecock of the Revolution." Bold, inflexible and passionately independent, he was inclined to be reckless in his use of military force. Placed in command of the South Carolina militia during the Revolution, he operated in the South, guerilla fashion, almost independent of the main army. Indeed, Cornwallis likened him to a "plague." After the war Sumter served for many years as congressman and senator from South Carolina, rounding out his career as United States Minister to Brazil (1809-1811). Attributed to Rembrandt Peale, circa 1795-1797. Independence National Historical Park Collection.

The British confused by the forests and swamps, unused to the climate and the tactics employed by the South Carolinians, soon fell prey to the wily Swamp Fox:

A moment in the British camp—
A moment—and away
Back to the pathless forest,
Before the peep of day.

IN January, 1782, there arrived in Charles Town aboard H.M.S. *Rotterdam,* Benjamin Thompson (1753-1814), an American born in Woburn, Massachusetts, but now a member of the King's American Dragoons. He was assigned to a "detachment of 200 horse, 500 infantry, and two pieces of artillery." Some of these men were the Volunteers of Ireland, a unit organized in Philadelphia that had first served under Lord Rawdon.

At the time of Thompson's arrival, the defiant legislature convened at Jacksonborough, twenty-five miles away, and Francis Marion had to temporarily leave his brigade to serve as a senator. His presence was necessary to form a quorum. Marion wrote to Colonel Peter Hörry on January 23, 1782, instructing him to send some of his calvary along the Wando River to Cainhoy, to be used in "cutting off the enemy's Horse which go out a foraging," and that "no boats or persons should pass from or to Charles Town without your or my passport."

Thompson—a fine military strategist—defeated Marion's men near the Santee. Soon afterward Thompson left for the North and in the spring of 1783 was in New York. By April he sailed for England, never to return to America. This New Englander, whose sojourn in South Carolina was to be a brief footnote to his career, was later knighted by George III and enobled by the Elector of Bavaria. As Count Rumford he founded the Royal Institution of Great Britain and is today remembered as one of the great early American scientists.

MORE serious and cruel than Clinton's proclamation was the order to the British commanders in South Carolina of the Marquess Cornwallis, who had taken over the Carolina command in June, 1780, ordering that "every militiaman, who has borne arms under the Crown and had afterwards joined the enemy, should be immediately hanged."

This unfortunate missive sealed the doom of the British in South Carolina. Guerilla warfare was stepped up, the patriot fervor was greater than ever, and hatred of the British reached new heights with the hanging of Colonel Isaac Hayne. The colonel, accepting the terms under which Charles Town surrendered, returned on parole to his plantation. After Clinton's decree Hayne was told he must at once become a British subject. Although his wife and several children were desperately ill, Hayne reported to Charles Town and was refused permission to return to his family unless he swore allegiance to Great Britain.

He objected to the clause that he "with arms . . . support the Royal Government," but was promised that such action on his part would never be required of him. When it was enforced, he declined to take up arms against his fellow Carolinians. Since the British had shown him little faith, had abrogated the terms of his parole and those under which his agreement with them was signed, he joined the colonials. The British, enraged, recaptured and sentenced him. When Hayne was hanged on July 18, 1781, it had a similar effect in Charles Town to the hanging of Nathan Hale in New York. The city knew what it could expect from the occupying forces. The light of liberty which had first been a small flame, then a brighter candle, was now more luminous than ever.

AFTER the American victories at King's Mountain (1780) and Cowpens (1781), and with Nathanael Greene's delaying tactics, the end came rather swiftly on October 19, 1781, with Lord Cornwallis's surrender to Washington, accompanied by Lafayette and the Comte de Rochambeau, at Yorktown. Surrender, however, did not mean the end of Charles Town's long hour of travail. Although orders to evacuate the city were issued on April 4, the city was not free of the British until they left in December, 1782. Charlestonians suffered accordingly. Many were seized and imprisoned in St. Augustine. When the British finally marched to their waiting vessels, they carried the plunder they had removed from Charles Town homes—furniture, paintings and plate—and, the final indignity, the bells of St. Michael's (which were later returned).

One of the tragedies of the final days of the Revolution was the death of John Laurens (1754-1782). Originally captured by Sir Henry Clinton when Charles Town fell to the British in 1780, he was exchanged and sent by the government in Philadelphia to enlist aid from France. He was not only highly successful in this endeavor, but endeared himself to the court of France, already enamored of another American, Benjamin Franklin.

Laurens returned and was present at Cornwallis's surrender. Once more in Carolina he was elected to the House of Representatives of the General Assembly. There were sporadic engagements between the Carolinians and the enemy, still occupying Charles Town and the surrounding countryside. At one of these, on August 27, 1782, at Tar Bluff on the Combahee River, Laurens was killed.

South Carolinians today remember with pride that America, according to John Adams, lost "its most prominent character." And that George Washington wrote: "He had not a

John Laurens (1754-1782). Valor, indeed rashness, characterized the short but brilliant career of the son of Henry Laurens. A lieutentant colonel on Washington's staff, he wounded Major General Charles Lee in a duel triggered by Lee's abuse of the Commander-in-Chief. Representing the army Laurens became "envoy-extraordinary" to France in 1780 and obtained substantial supplies for colonial forces. Yearning for the excitement of combat, he returned to this country, led a charge at Yorktown, then perished needlessly in an insignificant skirmish in his native South Carolina, August 27, 1782. Miniature on ivory by Charles Willson Peale, replica, circa 1784. Independence National Historical Park Collection.

fault that I ever could discover, unless intrepidy bordering on rashness could come under that denomination: and to this he was excited by the purest motives."

In a final break with the past—although Charlestonians have never been really known to do such a thing—Charles Town was incorporated in 1783 under the name Charleston. Charles Town denoted 113 years of progress from a frontier wilderness through a turbulent colonial period and a revolutionary break with Great Britain. Now, as Charleston, under a slightly different guise, it approached a period of less than a century, which would be in many ways its most historic, in some its most fruitful, and in one its most tragic.

IN the hot summer of 1787 the South Carolina delegation—Pierce Butler (1744-1822), Charles Pinckney (1757-1824), his cousin General Charles Cotesworth Pinckney (1746-1825) and John Rutledge (1739-1800)—made the long journey from Charleston to Philadelphia to spend weeks with their fellow delegates in hammering out a Constitution for the young republic. Butler was an aristocrat who championed the cause of the poor, disenfranchised settlers in the back country. That General Pinckney, soldier of the Revolution, was a staunch patriot is shown in his remark: "If I had a vein which did not beat with the love of my country, I myself would open it. If I had a drop of blood that could flow dishonourably, I myself would let it out!" The general was born on East Bay, a half a square above Market Street. Many years later his granddaughters granted land to the city for the market.

Catherine Drinker Bowen characterized his cousin when she wrote: "Years afterward, Charles Pinckney was to make extravagant claims concerning his plan and his part in the Federal Convention, managing thereby to earn for himself locally the nickname of Constitution Charlie." Rutledge had attended the Stamp Act Congress, the Continental Congresses and was later nominated as Chief Justice of the United States Supreme Court, but was never confirmed by the Senate.

William Jackson (1759-1828). An orphaned English immigrant, Jackson fortunately came under the guardianship of a well-known family. Benjamin Lincoln found Major Jackson a dependable aide-de-camp and assistant secretary of war (1782-1784). John Laurens entrusted Jackson with the shipment of war supplies (1781) and Alexander Hamilton's backing made him secretary of the Constitutional Convention. Washington, whom he respected most, employed him as his personal secretary from 1788 to 1791. Oil on ivory by unknown artist, 1793. Independence National Historical Park Collection.

IN Charleston today, on the handsome house at 94 Church Street, opposite both Cabbage Row and the Heyward-Washington House, a wooden tablet reminds the visitor that Theodosia Burr and her husband Governor Joseph Alston lived there. The house itself was built about 1730 and its earlier owner was Thomas Bee, a leader in the colonial government.

Theodosia, daughter of Vice-President Aaron Burr, re-

Gates and doorway of the Simmons-Edwards House, 14 Legaré Street, circa 1800. This property was acquired by Francis Simmons in 1800, and it is thought he built this "very handsome 'single' house upon it shortly thereafter." Simmons, who evidently had a cavalier attitude toward marriage, left his wife soon after their marriage and, according to Samuel Gaillard Stoney, "thereafter maintaining a casual though friendly acquaintance with her...." Marjorie R. Maurer photograph.

We are told that George Edwards sent a live oak acorn to serve as a model for the tall finials, but that the Italian marble cutters bound by custom used the conventional and traditional pineapple instead. Marjorie R. Maurer Photograph.

The Simmons-Edwards House from the garden. George Edwards acquired the property in 1816, two years after Simmons' death. "Tradition says," Stoney writes, "that he ordered this iron work and the elaborate marble cappings of his additions direct from Italy." Marjorie R. Maurer photograph.

mains one of the enigmatic heroines of American history. Beautiful, intellectual and far better educated than most men of her time, Theodosia married Alston and left her native New York for, as it turned out, a short life and residence in South Carolina. Her only child Burr Alston died in his tenth year in 1812.

In December of that year, mourning her son and already grieved by her father's fall from favor because of the Blennerhasset conspiracy, she sailed from Charleston aboard the *Patriot,* her destination New York and her father. Theodosia set sail in troubled seas, for it was the time of the War of 1812, and on that voyage she sailed into the unknown and into history as well. The *Patriot* was never again heard from. Legends abounded and persisted. The most popular—but never proven—was that Theodosia had been forced, with other passengers, to walk the plank. This story surfaced more than thirty years later when a dying seaman on the Outer Banks recounted it.

There are graves in Saint Helena's Churchyard in Beaufort, North Carolina, and Saint Paul's Graveyard in Alexandria, Virginia, that are said to be hers. Few reminders survive of Theodosia—a miniature here, a portrait by John Vanderlyn there, and the house at 94 Church Street in Charleston. But she, like Eliza Lucas Pinckney, is one of those legendary women who left their mark on Charleston and whose memory lingers on.

An uprising in 1822 dramatized certain undercurrents that lay beneath Charleston's apparent calm. It was, however, "the only really serious threat of servile insurrection which had threatened Charleston since that incited by the Spaniards at St. Augustine in 1739."

Denmark Vesey, who led it, had a highly romantic history and exotic origins. A mulatto of great personal beauty, he

The William Blacklock House, 18 Bull Street, circa 1800. *After the Revolution, when Charleston sought to recover from the ravages of British despoliation and occupation, the city slowly recovered its equilibrium and balance. The Blacklock House suggests the elegance of grand Charleston residences of the turn of the century. The line, balance and symmetry are evident in its façade. It is situated on a property large enough to give it a proper and balanced setting. Its architect is unknown but his sensitivity is evident in every line of this magnificent mansion.* HABS photograph by Louis I. Schwartz. Library of Congress.

was a protégé of a Captain Vesey, a slaver trading from St. Thomas to Santo Domingo. In 1800 after drawing fifteen hundred dollars in the East Bay Lottery, Vesey purchased his freedom for six hundred dollars, set himself up as a carpenter and accumulated a considerable estate. Apparently influenced by the Abolitionists in the North, he also resented his children's inheritance of slavery from their mothers. In touch with Abolitionists, and stirred by the events in Santo Domingo, where there had been a revolt, he began to lay plans for an uprising. Educated, and a powerful orator, he exhorted his people, identifying the Negroes with the Israelites.

Meetings were held and contributions for arms collected at his residence at 20 Bull Street. A blacksmith was engaged to make daggers, bayonets and pikes to be ready for the night of rebellion, when the governor and intendant would be killed, the Powder Magazine seized, buildings put to the torch, and the rebellious would confiscate what they could and leave by sea for the West Indies. It was said that word of the uprising was known by slaves from the Santee to Port Royal.

Vesey was betrayed by two house servants loyal to their owners and the following day a court of two magistrates and five freeholders, customary in South Carolina since colonial times in cases involving slaves, convened. On the night of June 22 Vesey was captured at the home of one of his wives (he had several). He engaged counsel, and ably defended himself, cross-examining witnesses with skill, but the testimony of informers threw the balance against him. He was condemned to be hanged as were thirty-six of those Negroes brought to trial. Twenty-nine others were sent out of state, and thirty-five were acquitted. Four whites—at least three of whom were foreign born—were tried in court of sessions for misdemeanor, fined and imprisoned.

Iron door in the Powder Magazine, 21 Cumberland Street. Erected circa *1713, it was used in the Revolution, but in 1780 when Sir Henry Clinton bombarded Charleston, the powder stored here was removed to a safer place.* Frances B. Johnston photograph, circa 1930. Library of Congress.

"The true extent of the conspiracy," we are told, "will never be known, for Vesey and his aides died without making revelations. In the face of the intense excitement that prevailed, it was considered remarkable that the customary machinery of the law functioned and that no unusual punishments were inflicted. The local newspapers kept quiet about the insurrection and referred only briefly to the trials."

In our own time Dorothy Heyward, widow of the author of *Porgy* and co-author with him of the book for *Porgy and Bess,* in 1948 dramatized the uprising in her play *Set My People Free.*

Soon after the uprising the Old Citadel on Marion Square was erected. Built as an arsenal, this sturdy old fortress was garrisoned by federal troops, then by state troops, until they were replaced in March, 1843, by twenty students who formed the first Corps of Cadets. (The legislature of South Carolina had on December 20, 1842, passed an act providing for the establishment of The Citadel, the South Carolina Military Academy.)

The huge golden eagle guards Bond Hall, main administration building of The Citadel. It was named for Colonel Oliver J. Bond, class of 1886 and president of the military college from 1908 until 1931. The Citadel has been in its present location, adjacent to Hampton Park, since 1922. The Citadel.

South Carolina Corps of Cadets on the quadrangle of the Old Citadel on Marion Square, December 23, 1892. Apparently the structure as it appears here resulted from an 1829 conversion of a building called the "tobacco inspection," which stood on this site a number of years earlier. The third floor, however, was not a part of the original conversion, but was added by 1850. The Citadel.

The Old Citadel on Marion Square dates from 1822 to 1910. In the former year the state legislature passed an "Act to Establish a competent Force to Act as a Municipal Guard for the Protection of the City of Charleston and its Vicinity," but it was not until 1829 that the Citadel was ready for occupancy. Shown here are the cadets on parade on Marion Square with the Old Citadel in the background. National Archives.

No returning hero in the history of the United States received a warmer, more emotional and more enthusiastic welcome than did the Marquis de Lafayette, when he toured America in 1824 and 1825, forty-three years after he played a vital role in the surrender of Yorktown. When Lafayette arrived to offer his services to General Washington, he was a youth of nineteen. On his return he was sixty-seven.

Every city and town he visited planned torchlight parades, fetes, official receptions, built triumphal arches in his honor, and accorded the aged nobleman the affection he deserved. Congress voted him a gift of land and two hundred thousand dollars. Charleston was no exception when it came to honoring the man. The entourage to escort him to the city included the Washington Light Infantry, the Fusiliers Françaises, the Society of the Cincinnati, dignitaries, school children and former soldiers and officers of the Revolution.

Lafayette's association with South Carolina went back to 1777, when he first set foot on American soil on North Island, near Georgetown. He lodged at the summer home of Major Benjamin Huger and there held Huger's young son, Francis Kinloch, on his knee.

The Nathaniel Russell House, 51 Meeting Street, circa 1809. No house in Charleston, and few in other cities of the United States, is more elegant than this jewel of a residence. Built for Nathaniel Russell, son of a chief justice of Rhode Island and a merchant who was known locally as "King of the Yankees," it was the work of "local mechanics [who] had a decade of experience with the light and airy manner made popular by Robert Adam." It has been called "the last great dwelling of the city's post-Revolutionary period." Robert W. Tebbs photograph. Library of Congress.

The oval music room in the Russell House is unique; there is no other like it in America. The windows open on a wrought-iron balcony, which follows the contours of the house on the second floor. The American Empire couch is circa 1810. Marjorie R. Maurer photograph.

The free-flying stair of the Nathaniel Russell House has been rightly called an "exercise in ellipses." Marjorie R. Maurer photograph.

The inner wall of the oval music room is enhanced by a pair of windows with mirrored panes. They not only balance the room beautifully, but they reflect images caught by time and eternity. Marjorie R. Maurer photograph.

The world outside as seen from a Palladian window. If the Russell House could be described in one word, airy would, perhaps, be the most judicious. This view is from a landing on the free-flying stair. Marjorie R. Maurer photograph.

In 1794 when Francis Huger was studying in Vienna, he learned of Lafayette's imprisonment at Olmütz. Concocting a scheme—impractical but highly romantic—of freeing Lafayette, he obtained a carriage and horses and enlisted the aid of Justus Erich Bollman. They freed the marquis, but at the border—which was also to prove such hazardous territory for Marie Antoinette—they were captured. Huger was imprisoned as well as Lafayette, but he managed to get a note to Thomas Pinckney, then United States minister in London, who effected his release.

On the Marquis de Lafayette's visit to Charleston he rode in the carriage with Francis Kinloch Huger, and when he greeted Thomas and Charles Cotesworth Pinckney, he embraced them French fashion, kissing them on both cheeks, much to the amusement of the onlookers. Lafayette's visit was a last distant echo of the Revolution.

CHARLESTON has always attracted its share of visitors and one who was in and out of the city during the 1830's and 1840's was John James Audubon (1785?-1851), the Santo Domingan-born naturalist. In Charleston he met a kindred spirit in the Reverend John Bachman, pastor of the Lutheran church and professor at the College of Charleston. He was also "an amateur, but skillful naturalist." Audubon, his assistant George Lehman and Henry Ward, his taxidermist, were guests of Dr. Bachman in his home on their first visit in 1831.

The Bachman home was used on that occasion as an office and headquarters by the naturalists. "Henry Ward skinned and preserved two hundred and twenty speciments of sixty different species of birds; Audubon drew fifteen birds; and Lehman completed five pictures by putting in the plants and landscapes for the backgrounds," Alexander B. Adams has written. Two Audubon sons married Bachman daughters; John to Maria, Victor to Mary Eliza.

First (Scots) Presbyterian Church, 57 Meeting Street, circa *1814. Although the present structure was completed in 1814, the first Scots Dissenters worshipped in the White Meeting House, where now stands the Circular Congregational Church. The church suffered damage from the earthquake of 1886, the tornado of 1938 and a fire in 1945.* HABS photograph by Louis I. Schwartz, 1962. Library of Congress.

SHOCKING EARTHQUAKES.

CHARLESTON, (S. C.) FEB 7, 1812.

Yesterday morning, about half past 3 o'clock the inhabitants of this place were very much alarmed by another tremendous shock of an Earthquake. About a minute before the shock commenced a loud subterraneous noise was heard resembling that made by a heavy loaded waggon running over frozen ground. The concussion began moderately, but soon became

extremely violent, continuing with sudden jerks. The houses continued to shake about 25 minutes, sometimes with such extreme violence that many were apprehensive of their falling down. One chimney was thrown down, and several bricks shook off of others; and several houses in town, were considerably cracked. The morning was perfectly calm; and had truly an awful appearance: the moon shone dimly, being surrounded by a circle, and cast a shade as if apparently eclipsed, which, together with the noise made by the trees in the woods, produced, in the minds of some, sensations totally indescribable. It was felt severely at Pittsburg, Penn. Flashes of light were seen in the S.W. A few nights before a brilliant ball, as large in appearance as the full moon, passed over the town from N. to S.

ETERNAL Power, who reigns in heaven above,
Whose attributes are justice, truth and love;
Whose parent care protects this earthly span;
And crowns with blessings vile ungrateful man,
Who ne'er unheeded, sees the sparrows fall,
But whose benevolence extends to all;
We bow before thy high and mighty throne,
And the dread justice of thy mandates own.

Creation owns thee as her sovereign Lord,
The changing seasons wait upon thy word,
Sun, moon and stars, their various stations fill,
Obedient to their mighty Maker's will,
At thy command the lightning's subtle power
In ruin lays the strong and lofty tower,
And the loud thunder's horror-striking sound,
Spreads pale dismay and terror all around.

At the Almighty's high and dread behest,
The trembling nation quakes from East to West,
All nature looks astonish'd at the sight.
When in the dark and dismal gloom of night,
The groaning earth in dire convulsive throes,
One awful scene of devastation shows;
Creation changes to a different face,
The rocks and mountains leave their wonted place

The watery lakes, in breadth, circumference large,
Now leave their beds by sudden, quick discharge,
The brooks and rivers by such powerful force,
O'erflow their banks and change their nat'ral
     course,
Men, women, children, fill'd with dread affright,
Transfix'd with horror, view the awful sight.
Some think the day of general doom is near,
Sounds of deep sorrow strike upon the ear,

The frantic mother shrieks in accents wild,
And to her bosom clasps her infant child;
The father, brother, and the virgin fair,
With mingled cries transpierce the wounded air!

If such the terror which these shocks inspire,
How will the sinner when the last dread fire
Shall burn the globe, before his Judge appear,
And the dire sentence of *Damnation* hear?
Then pealing thunders shall incessant roll,
And shake the trembling globe from pole to pole,
Sharp light'nings play through all the affrighted
     sphere,
And shooting downwards, set the world on fire.

The sea shall burn in that eventful day,
Rocks fall to dust, and mountains melt away,
The bursting flames in one grand column rise,
Curl o'er the earth and brighten all the skies.
Then rise the millions from the silent tomb;
And from their Judge hear their last final doom,
Some rise to happiness forever blest,
In the fair regions of eternal rest.

Others alas! sent to the shades below,
Will writhe in tortures of eternal woe,
Then while these warnings thunder in our ears,
Let's bear in mind that but a few short years,
Will intervene, before this beauteous world,
Shall in one moment be to ruin hurl'd.
Then mortals, bow beneath th' Almighty's rod,
Prepare, O! man, to meet an injur'd God.

BOSTON----PRINTED AND SOLD AT THE PRINTING-OFFICE, *Corner of Theatre-Alley.*

On subsequent visits Audubon drew the water birds that abounded on the sea islands, or in the marshy lands near the coast, in preparation for the second volume of *Ornithological Biography*. One of these was the long-billed curlew (*Numenius americanus*). In the background of the picture is a panoramic view of Charleston's low-lying skyline with Fort Sumter or Castle Pinckney visible. The naturalist himself recorded: "One beautiful November morning [in 1831] I left Charleston for a visit to Cole's Island, twenty miles distant. We . . . made ready for the arrival of the Long-billed Curlews at sunset."

ALTHOUGH Charleston's surface calm has often deceived the outsider, crisis has always been the warp and woof of her existence. True, the periods of crisis were punctuated with equal periods of calm. However, if it wasn't nature erupting—hurricanes, tidal waves and earthquakes, it was politics that inflamed passions and ruffled the city's serentiy. None was more disrupting than the events of 1832.

In that year South Carolina proclaimed the doctrine of nullification: that states could, if they chose, nullify any federal ordinance to which they objected. On November 24 South Carolina adopted the Ordinance of Nullification, which in turn was a declaration of states' rights.

The complexities and reasons for the situation were as obvious then as now. In 1832 tariffs were trebled on all woolen and cotton goods, iron, salt and certain other commodities— all essential to the South. Contrariwise, the duties on luxury items—coffee, tea and silk, not produced in New England,

Broadside, 1812, reporting the severity of a Charleston earthquake. Library of Congress.

Gravestone of James Legaré in St. Philip's Churchyard. James, son of Solomon and Amey, "departed this Life December 10th 1766 Aged 28 Years & 6 Mo." Mary C. Means photograph.

were reduced. The rural, agrarian South was to suffer at the hands of the manufactories of the North.

Carolinians were quick to declare themselves, and feelings ran high. The legislature protested, parades were held, speeches made and pamphlets on the subject were published. Friends and families took opposing sides and often split violently on the issue.

The answer was nullification—that individual states had the right to declare null and void and set aside any federal law which violated their voluntary compact under the Constitution. John C. Calhoun, the great South Carolinian, led the fight to have the legislature pass the Ordinance of Nullification.

The states' rights group—the "nullifiers"—took one side, among them Governor James Hamilton, Jr., Senator Robert Y. Hayne, Robert J. Turnbull and Calhoun. Turnbull wrote about nullification under the nom de plume of "Brutus." Opposing them were their fellow Charlestonians and Carolinians—the "unionists," which included Henry Middleton, Joel R. Poinsett, Colonel William Drayton, Huge S. Legaré, Daniel E. Huger and James L. Petigru. President Jackson had been asked to address the union meeting. Although he was not there in person, his letter was read to those in attendance:

Every enlightened citizen must know that a separation, could it be effected, would begin with civil discord and end in colonial dependence on a foreign power, an obliteration from the list of nations. But he should also see that high and sacred duties, which must and will at all hazards be performed present an unsurmountable barrier to the success of any plan or disorganization, by whatever patriotic name it may be decorated or whatever high feeling may be arrayed for its support.

Even Maria H. Pinckney, a granddaughter of Eliza, was moved to write "The Quintessence of Long Speeches, or a Catechism of State Rights." A convention called by the legislature met to settle the issue and oil troubled waters. It passed the Ordinance, nullifying the act increasing the tariffs, and declared no duties should be paid after February 1, 1833.

War, or at least some form of conflict, seemed imminent. President Jackson, a South Carolinian by birth, declared: "If the duties were not paid, the state would be reduced by force." General Winfield Scott was sent south in command of a body of troops, and a fleet was dispatched to Charleston as well.

Calhoun's voice was one of caution, patience and self-control, although allied with nullification. It was then that Henry Clay, the Great Compromiser, stepped into the breech with his compromise—that tariffs would be gradually reduced over a nine-year period—and the pride and feelings of both sides were assuaged. Conflict with the federal government was avoided for almost thirty years.

News of the controversy, heated as it was, was bound to be carried across the Atlantic. One adventurer who responded to the possibility of conflict was Edward John Trelawny (1792-1881), the romantic, swashbuckling friend of Byron and Shelley. "The mere prospect of war would not deter him. . . ." In fact, it acted as a goad. In early 1833 we find Trelawny in Charleston, describing—in a letter to Claire Clairmont, once Byron's mistress—its winter climate as preferable to that of China (where he had never been!).

It was during Trelawny's sojourn in Charleston that the work progressed on Fort Sumter, which would play a prominent role in the opening of the fratricidal conflict twenty-eight years later. Although it has never been conclusively proven that they met in Charleston, Trelawny was later to become intimate with Christian Edward Detmold, a "brilliant

Governor William Aiken House, 48 Elizabeth Street, circa 1817 and 1832. Aiken, a highly successful planter was governor of South Carolina from 1844 to 1846, and bought this residence in 1832. The main entrance hall, with its double ascending stair, confirms that the house "allowed for formal living on a magnificent scale and decorative treatment of a classical eclectic nature made it the most imposing residence of its period." HABS photograph by Louis I. Schwartz, 1958. Library of Congress.

young German-born engineer and industrialist, who was one of the builders of Fort Sumter."

A United States survey in 1826 suggested a series of fortifications along the coast, which would later be Fort Preble, Fort Warren, Narragansett Roads, Fort Monroe and Hampton Roads, Fort Moultrie, Castle Pinckney and Fort Sumter.

Earlier, on December 15, 1815, James Madison urged strong coastal defenses to prevent instances such as the burning of Washington by the British (1814): ". . . the character of the times . . . will sufficiently recommend to Congress a liberal provision for the immediate extension . . . of the works of defense . . . on our maritime frontier."

The Art Gallery in the Aiken House, often designated the Robinson-Aiken House because John Robinson, a factor, purchased the property in 1817 and apparently completed the dwelling by 1820. HABS photograph by Louis I. Schwartz, 1958. Library of Congress.

Fort Sumter was situated on a 2.4 acre shoal named for General Thomas Sumter. Building of the pentagon-shaped fortress began in 1829, but the major structural work wasn't completed until 1869. At least seventy thousand tons of granite and other rock, sand and shells had been used for the foundation. The walls, fifty feet above low water, were manned by 135 guns, with a complement of 650 men.

One of the soldiers stationed in 1829 at Fort Moultrie, opposite Fort Sumter, when the building of Sumter was just getting underway, was Edgar A. Perry, who was in reality Edgar Allan Poe. Later in his career he would hark back to the time on Sullivan's Island and the Isle of Palms as the setting for "The Gold Bug."

Few "necessaries" survive, probably because with the advent of interior plumbing such anachronisms were demolished. This one, photographed in 1963, belonged to the Aiken House and was situated in the northeast corner of the yard. HABS photograph by Louis I. Schwartz. Library of Congress.

Jail and Marine Hospital. Ballou's Pictorial, *August 8, 1857.* Library of Congress.

Lᴏɴɢ before the nullification crisis, and until his death in 1850, no South Carolinian was more prominent on the national political scene than John C. Calhoun. In 1811 he first went to Congress as a representative from the Abbeville district. It was he who introduced a bill to charter the second Bank of the United States, and he who supported the tariff bill of 1816.

President James Monroe appointed Calhoun to his cabinet as secretary of war, and he twice held the vice-presidency. In the election of 1824 he was elected to the office (182 electoral votes out of 260), and John Quincy Adams was the choice of the House of Representatives when no one candidate had a majority of electoral votes. Four years later he and Andrew Jackson, born in South Carolina but then a resident and a candidate from Tennessee, "in the first election decided entirely by popular vote . . . easily defeated the opposing ticket of John Quincy Adams and Richard Rush of Pennsylvania."

What began as entente gradually disintegrated to a point where both members of the executive branch were at odds with one another. All this revolved around and concerned a beautiful and voluptuous woman in whom neither was interested personally. Peggy O'Neill Timberlake, the wife of John Henry Eaton, secretary of war, was said to have been intimate with her husband before their marriage. Most Washington hostesses—including Floride Calhoun—would not receive her. The Vice-President upheld his wife; the President supported Eaton.

When the Ordinance of Nullification was passed, Robert

City of Charleston, South Carolina. Aquatint engraved by W. J. Bennett, 1853. Published by L. P. Clover, New York. Virtually every variety of seagoing vessel is pictured here, an indication of the importance of the port. Fort Moultrie can be seen at the extreme left. Library of Congress.

Second Presbyterian Church, Wragg Square, Charlotte and Elizabeth Streets, circa *1809-1811. Just a few steps from the Joseph Manigault House, the façade of this classically simple house of worship draws the wayfarer up its long path to the welcoming porch. Built by the architect-builders James Gordon (1783-1814) and John Gordon (1787-1835), the church has "a boldly projecting pediment and entablature supported by four engaged columns in the middle of the south side . . . ." This photograph taken in 1941 shows it before the disastrous fire of 1959, after which it was restored.* Robert W. Tebbs photograph. Library of Congress.

Y. Hayne resigned as senator from South Carolina. Nine weeks before the close of his second term as vice-president, Calhoun also resigned, the only man to do so until Spiro Agnew resigned in 1973.

Calhoun served in the Senate from 1832 until 1843 and from 1845 to 1850. In 1844 President John Tyler appointed him secretary of state, and it was Calhoun who in 1845 was instrumental in admitting Texas to the Union. However, President Polk did not include Calhoun in his cabinet and he again returned to private life. Daniel Elliott Huger of

Robert William Roper House, 9 East Battery, circa 1838. When this glorious house was built, nothing stood to the south to obscure the view from its portico to the Ashley River. After Roper died childless in 1851, and certain of his inherited wealth went according to his father's bequest to found the Roper Hospital, his widow sold the house. HABS photograph by C. O. Greene, 1940. Library of Congress.

The Fireproof Building, circa 1822-1827, seen from Washington Park, with the statue of William Pitt on the right. Originally designated the Mesne Conveyance Office, this elegant structure was designed by the architect Robert Mills (1781-1855). Mills had as his mentors Thomas Jefferson, James Hoban and Benjamin Henry Latrobe. No young architect could have done better. An appropriation in 1821 of $25,000 was made for the structure, and the site at Broad and Meeting Streets was purchased from the City Council of Charleston for $10,000. The Fireproof Building, as it has been known for most of its history, is now the home of the South Carolina Historical Society. Robert M. Tebbs photograph, 1937. Library of Congress.

Market Hall, 188 Meeting Street, circa 1841. Reminiscent of a Roman temple, it marks the spot on which between 1788 and 1804 was erected a public market. After the Civil War the hall housed the Confederate Museum. Now it is the center for interesting antique and craft shops, and a unique restaurant. Marjorie R. Maurer photograph, 1970.

Charleston, who had in 1843 been elected to succeed Calhoun, realizing Calhoun's value to South Carolina and in an act of unselfishness, resigned his seat in order to enable Calhoun to return to the Senate.

At Calhoun's death, although he was not a Charlestonian, Charleston asked that this distinguished Washington warrior be buried in South Carolina's most historic city. The *Charleston Yearbook* reported that "members of the Senate, the House of Representatives, and the Sergeant-at-Arms of the Senate, accompanied the bier." His body lay in state in City Hall. On April 26 "at early dawn, the bells of the city resumed their toll, business remained suspended, and a civic procession was formed. . . . The body was then borne by the guard of honor to the Western cemetery of the church within a structure of masonry, raised above the ground and lined with cedar wood."

Two of his bearers at his interment in St. Philip's churchyard were Henry Clay and Daniel Webster, both to die two years later. In keeping with the solemnity of the occasion, even the plametto trees were swathed in black. "The funeral cortege was the largest gathering of citizens ever seen in Charleston, occupying over two hours in passing any one point."

As in the case of so many, Calhoun did not rest in peace permanently. In 1863, after the evacuation of Morris Island by the Confederate forces, a group of Charlestonians, fearing Calhoun's body would be desecrated if the Union troops took the city, met at midnight in St. Philip's Churchyard and removed Calhoun's remains from the impressive tomb. First they "were conveyed to the Vestibule of the Church and placed under the stairs leading to the South Gallery." A piece of carpet was thrown over the box until the following night when a grave was opened in the eastern cemetery behind the church. There Calhoun lay until April 8, 1871, when John N. Gregg, the church sexton, identified the site of the secret burial and Calhoun's coffin was returned to its original tomb.

THE month of December, 1855, marked a theatrical event of international moment, but the actress herself was not aware that she was saying *au revoir* to the theatre. Nor was an indifferent Charleston. Rachel (1821-1858) had given her previous performance in Philadelphia's Walnut Street Theatre. The tuberculosis that would kill her was further aggravated by a heavy cold and she was coughing badly.

The company arrived on the first of December. "One thing is charming we have here! Real spring weather.

Everywhere, in the gardens, in the streets, even, we see roses in bloom, orange trees covered with fruit. It is delightful!"

Unhappily, when the box office opened, a "formidable fire broke out nearby" and four houses were destroyed. The prospective purchasers of tickets failed to turn up in large numbers, having been lured away by the fire, "one of the *grandes passions* of the American people!"

On December 10 at the New Charleston Theatre, Rachel's company—which included her sisters Sarah, Lia and Dinah—presented, without the star herself, *Le Depit*

Rachel, born Elisabeth Félix (1821-1858), the great French tragedienne who gave her last performance in Charleston. Lithograph de Maurin, rue de Vaugirard 72, Paris. Author's collection.

The Charleston Story

127

The Mills House was known as the Hotel St. John when it was photographed here in 1905. The hotel opened in 1853 and was built by Otis Mills, who made his fortune in grain and real estate. Detroit Publishing Company photograph. Library of Congress.

Amoureaux, Les Droits De L'Homme and *Le Chapeau D'Un Horloger*. The house was poor, but three days later they gave *Tartuffe*. Léon Beauvallet, one of her troupe, wrote: "As we gave tickets to all the cooks at our hotels, and as these cooks are all French, the piece had a stunning success."

A china statue of Rachel was exhibited in the French China Depot, 118 King Street, and on Monday, December 17, this supreme exponent of Racine and Moliere, gave her last performance in any theatre in *Adrienne Lecouvreur*.

Léon Beauvallet's Gallic prose is excessive in *Rachel and the New World*: "She is not quite well; she still has this accursed cough, which will not leave her; but, at last, she resolves to play in spite of it, and she does play!

"Unfortunately, she plays tonight *for the last time* in America.

"On the bills the public are notified that Rachel would give *one* night—a *single* night—and that *positively*. The management did not think that it was speaking so truly."

C ATASTROPHE in the battle dress of war was at hand, but Charleston in the late 1850's was much like Paris just before Waterloo, Vienna in the twilight of the Habsburgs or the Congress of Vienna when Europe danced to the strains of a false waltz. Charleston was gay, prosperous, rich and powerful, but the specter of tragedy was reflected in the mirrors of its drawing rooms although the inhabitants were not aware of the enemy at hand.

The Charleston Story

129

It does not seem at all coincidental that the heroes of two of the most enduring novels contemporary America has produced—*Show Boat* by Edna Ferber (1926) and *Gone With the Wind* by Margaret Mitchell (1936) bore Charleston names of this enchanted, but doomed period: Gaylord Ravenal and Rhett Butler. Congress danced! The old order changed. But only some elements of the South were conscious of this. In this last stand of chivalry, those descendants of the immigrants of the *Carolina* and *Port Royal* stood firm for the principles on which Charleston and the South throve and survived.

Views from St. Michael's Church, looking toward the Exchange and the Cooper River, at the time of the Civil War. Library of Congress.

Charleston in 1860 was in an unique position. This small, self-contained city, not yet two hundred years old, was in many ways the idealized city of the Old South. This could not be said in all honesty of New Orleans, for it was a newer, younger city (1718), and Louisiana had only entered the Union in 1812 after the Louisiana Purchase (1803).

Calhoun, Clay and Webster—those giants of the Congress who were never elected President—were gone. The century, although not on the wane was past its midpoint, and those festering sores—states' rights and slavery—were such that a surgeon's lancet was needed. The doctrine of secession was an underlying issue. Emancipation would come later. Abolition had been a point of contention for the better part of thirty years, ever since William Lloyd Garrison had founded *The Liberator* (1831) and alerted the northern liberals to the evils of slavery. The Grimké sisters—Angelina Emily (1805-1879) and Sarah Moore (1792-1873)—of Charleston were two of the most ardent Abolitionists.

This sea of ferment surrounded and permeated the small city of Charleston in 1860. The Democratic Convention met

North Eastern View of Charleston with North Eastern Rail Road. Drawn from Nature by Wm. Keenan. Entered According to act of Congress in the Clerks office for Charleston District. Lithographed and published by Wm. Keenan, 250 King cor. Hasel Street. Circa 1860's. Library of Congress.

The watermelon market. From Frank Leslie's Illustrated Newspaper, *December 15, 1866.* Library of Congress.

there in that year and South Carolina immediately threatened to secede from the Union if an antislavery President was elected. It is generally forgotten that James Buchanan of Pennsylvania, and not Abraham Lincoln of Illionois, was president when the crisis began that lengthened into the Civil War.

On December 17, 1860, at a convention held at Columbia, South Carolina, a committee was called to draw up the Ordinance of Secession. The convention, because of the danger of smallpox, moved to Charleston where the Reverend John Bachman, Audubon's old friend, opened it with a prayer. Its

The Roman Catholic Cathedral of St. John and St. Finbar before the fire of 1861. The residence with the elaborate ironwork is the John Rutledge House, 116 Broad Street, which dates prior to the Revolution. The wrought iron is by Christopher Werner, and certain changes were made to the façade by a nineteenth-century architect. Library of Congress.

final session was held in St. Andrew's Hall. There the delegates voted to adopt the Ordinance. Its signing on December 20 in the South Carolina Institute Hall was on a table used for the ratification of the Constitution of the United States in 1788; a chair used by General David F. Jamison, president of the convention, had first come to Charleston in 1720. Today it is in the Charleston Museum.

On the night of December 26, when Charleston was still recovering from Christmas and was, in some manner, unaware, Major Robert Anderson sent the women and children from Fort Moultrie on Sullivan's Island to Fort Johnson on James Island. And then, quietly and without suspicion he moved his garrison to Fort Sumter. Assistant Surgeon S. W. Crawford, who was a member of the garrison at Fort Moultrie, afterward described this in *The Genesis of the Civil War:*

> *Shortly after dusk the movement began. The sea was still, the moon shining brightly. Three six-oared barges and two four-oared boats were in readiness on the beach below the fort. . . . The men entered the three boats awaiting them silently and in order. Their arms were so disposed as to avoid attracting attention in the bright moonlight.*

Robert Molloy tells us: "When the news [of secession] was given out, the crowds wearing palmetto cockades, cheered themselves hoarse; bands played; artillery salutes were fired; bells were rung. . . . A *Te Deum* was sung at the Cathedral of St. John and St. Finbar, and all the churches rejoiced; pitch was burned in the streets." Following this a commission was dispatched to Washington, D. C., to negotiate the surrender of Forts Sumter, Johnson, Moultrie and Castle Pinckney. Secession did nothing to lessen passions. The oratory and journalism were extravagant and purple in their intensity.

During the weeks before the shelling of Fort Sumter, Charlestonians felt great admiration for the small band of men stubbornly holding onto the bit of federal property in their harbor. Supplies were offered to them, which they politely refused. Among the garrison was Captain Abner Doubleday who, after the war, would be remembered not for his gallantry and bravery in service, but because he originated baseball.

If the signing of the Ordinance of Secession was in Charleston the most important event of 1860, April 12 was the crucial date of 1861. It was almost a century after Concord Bridge that the shot fired was *again* heard round the world.

The shelling of Fort Sumter was, and is, one of the dramatic moments of American history. Major Robert Anderson, whose father took part in the defense of Fort Moultrie (then Fort Sullivan) during the Revolution, and his men heroically stood their ground.

After more than thirty-four hours under fire, with no help from the federal ships stationed beyond the bar, Major Anderson and his garrison surrendered. E. Milby Burton described Sumter by saying "the fort itself looked exhausted, too; it appeared as if 'the hand of the destroying angel had swept ruthlessly by and left not a solitary object to relieve the general desolation.' The parapet was a wreck, the parade ground was pitted with shell craters, and the barracks had been gutted by fire. . . ."

White Point Gardens, today referred to as the Battery, became the stage box as Charlestonians, the spectators, watched the drama of the Civil War begin. The stage was Fort Sumter; curtain time 4:30 A.M. The weather was dark and cloudy with sunrise at 5:37 and a heavy mist covered the harbor.

Interior of Secession Hall. The date of the photograph (a stereoptican view) is unknown, but the fashions date it immediately after the Ordinance of Secession in 1860 and before it was destroyed in the fire of 1861.   Library of Congress.

Fort Sumter in 1903.   Underwood & Underwood photograph. Library of Congress.

Fort Sumter presented a forlorn, neglected picture in 1901.   Detroit Publishing Company photograph. Library of Congress.

"The firing of the mortar awoke echoes from every nook and corner of the harbor and in this dead hour of night, before dawn, that shot was a sound of alarm that brought every soldier in the harbor to his feet, and the city of Charleston from their beds," observed Captain Stephen D. Lee, aide-de-camp to General P. G. T. Beauregard, the Confederate commander in Charleston. "A thrill went through the whole city. It was felt the Rubicon was passed. . . ."

The *New York Herald* for April 13 reported:

> *Civil War has at last begun. A terrible fight is at this moment going on between Fort Sumter and the fortifications by which it is surrounded.*

> *. . .at twenty-seven minutes past four o'clock this morning Fort Moultrie began the bombardment by firing two guns. To these Major Anderson replied with three of his barbette guns, after which the batteries on Mount Pleasant, Cummings Point, and the Floating Battery, opened a brisk fire of shot and shell.*

> *Breaches [in Fort Sumter], to all appearance, are being made in the several sides exposed to fire. Portions of the guns there mounted have been shot away.*

It is not improbably that the fort will be carried by storm.

The soldiers are perfectly reckless of their lives, and at every shot jump upon the ramparts, observe the effect, and then jump down, cheering.

The excitement of the community is indescribable. With the very first boom of the gun thousands rushed from their beds to the harbor front, and all day every available place has been thronged by ladies and gentlemen, viewing the solemn spectacle through their glasses. Most of these have relatives in the several fortifications, and many a tearful eye attested to the anxious affection of the mother, wife, and sister, but not a murmer came from a single individual.

The spirit of patriotism is as sincere as it is universal. Five thousand ladies stand ready to respond to any sacrifice that may be required of them.

In Charleston at the time, a medical student named Joseph Adrian Booth served as a doctor to the Confederates. He was a brother of John Wilkes Booth, whose assassination of President Lincoln in 1865 would so affect the Reconstruction Era and the fate of cities such as Charleston.

As night fell on the city, rain provided a curtain between the Battery and Fort Sumter. In the morning when the rain stopped, the spectators could see that Sumter was on fire. Continued resistance was useless.

Anderson accepted terms and the bombardment stopped. When he and his men boarded the *Isabel,* a steamer provided for them by Beauregard, to be taken to the *Baltic,* a ship of the Union fleet beyond the bar, a scene was enacted that shows

Citadel cadet John E. Boinest, a corporal in Company A of the Corps of Cadets in December, 1864, when he was a junior at the military college, which was also known as the South Carolina Military Academy. The Citadel.

the respect felt for each other by the combatants on both sides. As the *Isabel* slowly steamed past Morris Island, the Confederate soldiers with heads uncovered stood along the beach as Major Anderson and his gallant men passed before them.

CHARLESTON has always been a stage setting for history, and has lent itself admirably to this role. In 1861 it achieved its finest hour. Four long years of war stretched before it. Charleston, which had rung up the curtain on the drama of the War between the States would ring it down just before Appomattox, which became almost an anticlimax to the events in South Carolina. The trauma that resulted would never be absent from its psyche afterward, would determine its course in history for seventy-five years, and would mold its character.

Now that war was a reality, the Union controlled the entire coast from Georgetown, South Carolina, to New Smyrna, Florida, with the exception of Charleston. By April 19, 1861, President Lincoln had issued orders to blockade all southern ports. The frigate *Niagara* arrived on May 11 to be the first blockading vessel to carry out the order.

By November, 1861, Port Royal had fallen and Charleston was thrown into panic. The enemy was at hand, there were traitors within, the city would be burned, sacked! On November 5 Robert E. Lee, who was in command of South Carolina, Georgia and East Florida, arrived in the city and informed Brigadier General Roswell S. Ripley that defenses were to be thrown up on Charleston Neck as soon as possible. At all costs the Charleston and Savannah Railroad was to be kept intact.

Ruins seen in 1865 from the Circular Congregational Church on Meeting Street. Library of Congress.

3448

Ruin of the Circular Congregational Church just after the Civil War. Library of Congress.

Fire and bombardment succeeded in leveling many of Charleston's noble structures. This view of Meeting Street shows the scaffolded Circular Congregational Church with St. Michael's in the distance. The Mills House is on the right. U.S. War Department General Staff photograph in the National Archives.

It wasn't the enemy, but again fire that first devastated the city. And, at that, it was carelessly caused when some slaves were cooking over an open fire. At the time General Lee was dining at the Mills House. The fire spread quickly, leaping from one building to the next, and before it was extinguished the Pinckney House at the corner of East Bay and Ellery Street, the Rutledge House on Tradd Street, the South Carolina Institute Hall where the Ordinance of Secession was signed, the Circular Congregational Church, the Charleston Theatre, the Apprentices' Library and St. Andrew's Hall were destroyed, as were most of the paintings in the Carolina Art Association. The Cathedral of St. John and St. Finbar (where people had stored goods, thinking it fireproof) was another victim, and Legaré Street to Tradd and both sides of Broad Street were also burned out.

The scene was one of utter desolation, with few buildings standing among the ruins. In all 540 acres were burned and hundreds were homeless. At the height of the conflagration people were seen carrying furniture and other belongings to safety, often to find that these hiding places were burned as well. From all over the South people responded to the tragedy, sending money to help the homeless. Food came in from the Low Country plantations.

Charleston settled down to war and settled in to withstand the blockade. By December, 1861, the "Stone Fleet," heavily ballasted ships no longer seaworthy, were sunk by the

The devastation of Charleston was extreme, following the fire of 1861, but the morale of its citizens remained high. Here the ruins of the Circular Congregational Church are seen in the foreground with the steeple of St. Philip's in the background. U.S. War Department General Staff photograph in the National Archives.

The Cathedral of St. John and St. Finbar after the fire of 1861. This scene at the corner of Broad and Legaré Streets was taken in 1865. U.S. Department General Staff photograph in the National Archives.

Federals in Charleston harbor, and the following month four-
teen additional vessels met the same fate. However, nature
took its own course and high tides and strong winds carved
out new channels for the blockade runners to use.

   The Governor and Council passed a resolution "that
Charleston should be defended at any cost of life and property,
and that in their deliberate judgment they would prefer a
repulse of the enemy with the entire city in ruins to an evacuation or surrender of any terms whatever." This was affirmed
when General Lee wrote to Major General John C. Pemberton, who commanded the district, that he was to defend the
city and if necessary it was "to be fought street by street and
house by house as long as we have a foot of ground to stand
on." With this in mind Captain William H. Echols, the chief
engineer, was ordered to conceive a plan for defending the
city's streets and public squares.

Hibernian Hall in April, 1865. U.S. Signal Corps photograph (Brady Collection) in the
National Archives.

*O'Connor House, 180 Broad Street, April, 1865. Federal officers were
confined here under fire.* Library of Congress.

THE long siege began. Union forces were repulsed at the Battle of Secessionville on James Island (1862). Fort Sumter, now garrisoned by Confederate forces, was to be bombarded constantly—three times heavily and for long periods—and at one point its defenders managed to hold off Federal forces with no more than four Wentworth shoulder rifles mounted with telescopic sights. The garrison never surrendered and its heroic story is one of the most stirring in American military annals.

On August 16, 1863, the first great bombardment of the fort began, and when General Quincy A. Gillmore demanded the evacuation of both Fort Sumter and Morris Island, General P. T. G. Beauregard, with all the courtesy of the Old South, replied that "neither the works on Morris Island nor Fort Sumter will be evacuated on the demand you have been pleased to make." On August 24 Gillmore informed General Halleck in Washington: "Fort Sumter is today a shapeless and harmless mass of ruins." It might well have been—5,009 projectiles weighing over 500,000 pounds were thrown at the island fortress in a seven-day period—but Sumter remained invincible, an infantry outpost between Charleston and the menacing blockading fleet beyond the bar. When Admiral J. A. Dahlgren demanded its surrender, Major Stephen Elliot replied: "Inform Admiral Dahlgren that he may have Fort Sumter when he can take it and hold it."

Charlestonians, despite the privations and restrictions the war put upon them, showed a lively interest in its progress as seen from White Point Gardens, where a Blakely gun

St. Philip's Church, target for the Union batteries on Morris Island. The Planters' Hotel (now the Dock Street Theatre) is on the left, the Huguenot Church to the right. U.S. War Department General Staff photograph in the National Archives.

was mounted. The roar of the guns sent hundreds of citizens there to watch, while others stationed themselves on the housetops. The Charleston *Courier* reported on September 3, 1863, that "the whole horizon at times seemed to be on fire," when broadsides from the Yankee *New Ironsides* were leveled against the city.

As summer of 1863 came to a close, there were twenty-two thousand Union men on Morris and Folly islands and Admiral Dahlgren's fleet was there beyond Fort Sumter where, according to Charlestonians, the Ashley and Cooper Rivers formed the Atlantic Ocean. Spies were constantly in and out of the city, and the Union commanders were able to learn troop movements and other vital information from simply reading the Charleston newspapers.

Torpedo warfare began, and in October, 1863, the torpedo ram *Little David* left the harbor and rammed the U.S.S. *New Ironsides*. By the twenty-sixth of the month the harbor and its vicinity were wracked with the deafening roar of cannon,

The Little David, *one of the first torpedo boat-submarines to be employed by the Confederates against the Union navy.* U.S. War Department General Staff photograph in the National Archives.

Officers and men of the ironclad Passaic *at divine service.* U.S. Signal Corps photograph (Brady Collection) in the National Archives.

Earthworks in 1865 on lower Meeting Street, looking north from South Battery. The earthworks in the middle of the street were possibly part of the city's inner ring of defenses. U.S. War Department General Staff photograph in the National Archives.

which continued for forty-one days and nights. The second great bombardment of Fort Sumter had started. Of particular sorrow to Charleston were the deaths of thirteen members of the city's Washington Light Brigade, who were crushed to death when the barracks roof on Sumter fell in. St. Michael's church sustained many hits, its chancel and organ were wrecked, and the roof of the South Carolina Society Hall was damaged. Many citizens left the city and those who remained moved further uptown out of range of the guns.

During this period, President Jefferson Davis visited Charleston and delivered "an eloquent and patriotic address" at City Hall. What is even more noteworthy is that at that time he and General Beauregard were barely speaking! Christmas night was the worst night of the bombing when 134 shells fell, starting fires in the city, one at the corner of Church Street and St. Michael's Alley. But on New Year's Day, 1864, silence reigned. Not a shot was fired on either side.

Earlier an incident occurred at Sumter, reminiscent of the Revolutionary one at Fort Moultrie. On November 27, seeing the flag had been shot down, Private James Tupper, Jr., of the 27th South Carolina Volunteers, and some fellow soldiers replaced it while under constant fire for at least fifteen minutes. When they had successfully raised it, showing that they had not lost their sense of humor even under fire, two of the group politely tipped their caps to the gunners on Morris Island.

By December 2 it was apparent even to Admiral Dahlgren that the men on Sumter were invincible. He confessed in his diary: "It is admitted now that the Rebels are snug in the ruins. Shot and shell will not drive them out." A week after the second bombardment ended Fort Sumter was hit by an explosion—internal in character—of such severity that "it nearly caused its evacuation." All Charleston watched with pride as Sumter weathered everything the Union forces directed its way. It looked, according to Major John Johnson, reporting later, more like "a volcanic pile" than a fortification.

I F it wasn't the bombardment of Fort Sumter that kept Charleston on its mettle, it was the fire of long-range guns into the city. Charlestonians were not complacently weathering the siege; the activity within the city was intense. In addition to the *Little David,* there was the *Hunley,* a torpedo ram which sank on several occasions during its trial runs, only to sink forever with seven men when it dived under the *Indian Chief,* a Union receiving ship. However, it was responsible for the sinking of the U.S.S. *Housatonic.*

The resourcefulness and inventiveness of the men who constructed these torpedo boats—forerunners of modern submarines—was nothing short of ingenious. In addition to the excitement of the torpedo runs, there were the arrivals and departures of the blockade runners themselves. Prior to July 10, 1863, the blockade was imperfect enough that vessels entered the port of Charleston and departed with impunity at little or no risk. An active trade with Nassau brought in necessary supplies, and as late as January 20, 1865, these blockade runners were still successfully eluding the Union navy.

It is difficult today to understand how Charleston managed to survive even with the goods brought in by blockade runners. By early 1862 there was a shortage of shoes, and in the spring of 1863 corn was selling for $225 a bushel and bacon for $1.00 a pound. As the war dragged on, things became even worse. Bacon, in 1864, sold for $5.00 a pound, butter for $6.00, sugar for $8.00, a fresh shad went for $10.00, and tea—again reminiscent of the Revolution—brought between $15.00 and $25.00 a pound. Salt was at a premium, and when a ship did arrive its contents were quickly auctioned to the townspeople.

Bed sheets were scarce, and wounded and ill soldiers— there was an epidemic of yellow fever in October, 1864—were covered with carpets and rugs. Women stayed up all night

The Battery and East Bay in 1865. The state of siege, indicated by the guns, was the longest an American city endured.   U.S. War Department General Staff photograph in the National Archives.

The gates of Old Goose Creek Plantation opened on the traditional avenue of live oaks fringed with Spanish moss. Underwood & Underwood photograph, 1903. Library of Congress.

sewing cartridge bags, and able-bodied men under cover of darkness transported bags of sand to bolster the defenses of Fort Sumter.

Gallantly Charleston put on a good face for itself and the world. A semblance of social life continued and even parties were given at Fort Sumter when there was a lull in the bombardment. To help bolster the men's morale, steamboats filled with ladies, accompanied by either General Beauregard or General Ripley, sailed over to the battered island.

It was the opinion of the Union army that "to capture Richmond would be grand, but to capture Charleston would be glorious." Still the Cradle of Secession held out. For sixty days and nights—from July 7 to September 8, 1864—the third bombardment of Fort Sumter continued. In all 14,666 rounds were fired at it, and at the same time five simultaneous attacks were made on the perimeter of Charleston. After three weeks bombardment Admiral Dahlgren, who had watched Charleston—the prey he could not capture—from the fleet, astutely observed: "The northeast front still stands erect, and the work is nearly impregnable." The Yankees could not help but feel admiration for the men in grey. Colonel W. W. H. Davis of the 104th Pennsylvania bore out Dahlgren's verdict, when he wrote: ". . .the tenacity with which the enemy held on to Sumter was wonderful."

But among the military there was bitterness, too, against the city that had withstood everything they had thrown against it, and endured. Major General Henry W. Halleck, chief of staff in Washington, wrote to General Sherman: "Should you capture Charleston, I hope that by some accident the place may be destroyed, and if a little salt shall be sown upon its site it may prevent the growth of future crops of nullification and secession."

Fortunately, Sherman did not try to capture Charleston. If after nearly four years the Union army and navy had been unable to take the city, he would not endeavor to do so, though other parts of the state suffered his torch. He replied to Halleck: "The truth is the whole company is burning with insatiable desire to wreak vengeance upon South Carolina. I almost tremble at her fate."

THE foundations of the Confederacy were crumbling, and the time for withdrawal came at last. On the night of February 17-18, 1865, all the agony of four years defense came to an end. Cotton piled high in the city's squares, in anticipation of this moment, was set afire as were thousands of bushels of rice. Even the bridge across the Ashley was on fire. The Blakely gun in White Point Gardens was blown up and fires broke out throughout the city. Charleston, the child of catastrophe, was burning. Fire had been as much a part of its history as had rice, cotton and indigo, or the men and women who planted and exported it.

Explosions—the magazine on Sullivan's Island and the Northeastern Railroad depot both went up—occurred as

Exploded 600-pound Blakely gun at White Point Battery. The gun was intentionally damaged in February, 1865, to prevent it falling into Union hands when the city was evacuated. U.S. War Department General Staff photograph in the National Archives.

darkness gave way to morning. The explosion at the depot caused the deaths of 150 people. The terror continued as three vessels—the *Palmetto State,* the *Chicora* and the *Charleston* exploded. The city was afire from river to river, something the combined might of the Union army and navy had not been able to accomplish. It was time at last for the Confederate troops to evacuate and the Union army to take possession of the city. Then the looting began. The soldiers of the 21st U.S. Colored Troops, who controlled the city, began a systematic breaking in of houses, taking what they wanted as they cursed and berated the dwellers. The Miles Brewton House at 27 King Street became the headquarters for this group and the 127th New York Volunteers, who garrisoned the city under Brigadier General Alexander Schimmelfennig. No attempt was made to stop the soldiers from taking what they wanted. After four years of privation and siege, Charleston had to stand by and see its homes stripped of furniture, pictures and silver, whatever happened to take the soldiers' fancy.

The record of the looting is a public one; officers were as guilty as common soldiers. The treasures of Charleston were shipped north to grace homes there. Charleston was as desolate, as devastated as any destroyed European city after World War II. The wind blew through bleak stretches where not a building stood. Bricks and burned timbers lay everywhere with only a fugitive flower or a bit of grass struggling for life among them. The lovely gardens were trampled, neglected and gone. Charleston was a city of ashes. Yet from those ashes it would, phoenix-like, rise again—and this time gloriously.

T HE war was over at last and Charleston thought only of rebuilding. There was one last act, however, which when played out would round out history and complete the circle. On April 14, 1865—four years to the day the rebels compelled

Ceremonies at Fort Sumter on April 14, 1865, when the flag was again raised. Henry Ward Beecher gave the address. In spite of bitterness over the outcome of the war, most of Charleston observed the ceremonies either at Fort Sumter, from the Battery or on boats in the harbor. National Archives Gift Collection.

Major Robert Anderson to strike the Stars and Stripes from the flag staff at Fort Sumter—Anderson, now a general, stood on the spot and raised the same torn and battered flag over the ruins of the fort.

All Charleston witnessed the ceremony—from the Battery, from the housetops, and from the flag-decorated ships and boats which filled the harbor. Great crowds thronged Fort Sumter itself to hear Henry Ward Beecher deliver the oration. He reminded his listeners that "We raise our fathers' banner. . .that it may heal all jealousies, unite all policies, inspire a new national life, compact our strength, purify our princi-

ples, enable our national ambitions, and make this people great and strong. . .for the peace of the world. . . ."

The signal was given, cannon boomed, the band played "The Star-Spangled Banner," and General Anderson ran the flag up to stay, as one writer observed: "A perpetual menace to treason from within, or to foreign enemies from without."

FIRE, storm, flood, hurricane and earthquake have been Charleston's lot throughout her long life. The events beginning on Tuesday, August 31, 1886, were the worst the small city was to suffer since the Civil War. The *Charleston Yearbook* reported:

> *The streets of the city were silent and nearly deserted. Overhead, the stars twinkled with unwonted brilliancy in a moonless, unclouded sky. The waters of the wide harbor were unruffled by not even a passing breeze. Around the horizon the dark woodlands hung like purple curtains shutting out the world beyond, as though nature itself guarded the ancient city hidden within the charmed circle. Earth and sea alike seemed wrapped in a spell of hushed and profound repose, that reflected as in a mirror the quiet of the blue eternal heavens bending over all.*

The first shock was felt about 9:51 P.M., with a second one soon afterward at 9:59. In all there were four severe shocks before midnight, three others at 2:00 A.M., 4:00 A.M. and 8:30 A.M. on September 1. Every home in the city was broken or shattered in some way, and walls and partitions swayed. Throughout the night were heard shrieks, cries of pain and terror, shouts and prayers, and the crash of falling masses of stone, brick and mortar. A wailing crazed with fear hovered over the city and worst of all there was the shout of "Fire!"

As night wore on "The air itself was strangely still. In the writer's [Carl McKinley's] garden an unprotected lamp burned until four o'clock, or later, with a flame that did not once waver. All nature seemed to be waiting in breathless suspense for the issue of the hour, of the next minute, the next moment."

The earthquake of 1886 damaged many public buildings, such as the Old Guard House and Police Station at Broad and Meeting Streets. After it was razed the Post Office replaced it on the site. Heliotype Printing Company, Boston, photograph. Print and Picture Department, Free Library of Philadelphia.

The corner of Atlantic Wharf and Exchange Street, following the earthquake. Heliotype Printing Company, Boston, photograph. Print and Picture Department, Free Library of Philadelphia.

Daylight brought reality. "Every house was in worse condition than had been suspected." The steeple of St. Michael's was, fortunately, not injured, but the station house opposite had lost its parapet and the portico and pillars of Hibernian Hall had crashed. In all nearly twenty buildings were burned. These tragedies were ignored by a dazed populace, waiting for further manifestations of the earthquake.

Bethel Methodist Church, Calhoun and Pitt Streets, circa 1852-1853. While the architect is not anonymous, his identity remains vague–"a Mr. Curtis." It is supposed he was James M. Curtis, who designed the Joseph Aiken House. The Greek Doric temple withstood the shocks of the earthquake of 1886, and today lends elegance to the city. HABS photograph by C. O. Greene, 1940. Library of Congress.

Invalids were brought out on mattresses, the dead and injured carried to parks and squares. Forty-nine persons died of injuries and seven from exposure. There was no lack of food, but there was limited means of preparing it. A general fear was felt that a tidal wave would follow the earthquake and cover the entire peninsula.

Tremors recurred for one or two days afterward, and the citizens were prepared for another earthquake to follow. Sailors came ashore to help and the railroads offered free transportation to those who could not pay their way.

"Thousands of blacks and whites alike—no difference was recognized and no discrimination shown—were the recipients of the bounty of their more fortunate fellow-citizens, who proved to be neighbors in the hour of misfortune."

The statistics, when finally gathered, were staggering. Not more than a half dozen houses escaped injury, and one quarter of the buildings on Charleston Neck were demolished. A Board of Inspectors examined 6,956 buildings, and found ninety percent were injured more or less, while frame buildings suffered from fallen chimneys. "Not 100 out of 14,000 chimneys escaped damage, and 95 percent of these . . . were broken off at the roof and went to the ground."

The Charleston Light Station on Morris Island reported it counted eighteen shocks up to the evening of September 1, although not more than ten had been counted in the city. (The height of the tower and the nature of the island's soil caused it to respond to vibrations not generally felt in Charleston.) There was a non-scientific report recorded as well. "Prince," half St. Bernard, half Newfoundland, belonging to J. B. Kershaw in Camden, 112 miles away, was reported to have felt the tremors before they actually came.

It took Charleston months to recover, to clean the city, to repair the houses and gardens, but from the beginning Charleston has been blessed with hope. It had recovered from the Civil War, twenty years before, gone through the long era of Reconstruction, and suffered countless tragedies before caused by the forces of nature. A new city arose as new ones had done for over two hundred years.

King Street looking north from Hasell Street, circa 1912. There was a sense of improved commercial activity and much of the outward poverty of the post-Civil War period had disappeared. Detroit Publishing Company photograph. Library of Congress.

King Street in 1891 shows the apparent prosperity of the city after the devastating earthquake five years before. B. W. Kilborn photograph. Library of Congress.

IN 1905 one of America's most distinguished expatriates, Henry James, returned to his native heath. In a series of visits that would result in *The American Scene,* "The Master" saw Boston, Providence, New York, Philadelphia, Baltimore and Richmond before arriving at Charleston. "To arrive at Charleston early in the chill morning," he wrote, "was to appear to have come quite adventurously far, and yet to be not quite clear about the grounds of the appearance."

In 1912 Church Street below Tradd showed all the signs of neglect that the city suffered following the Civil War and the earthquake. Number 71, the Colonel Robert Brewton House, circa 1730, is the earliest example of what is known in Charleston as a "single house." Brewton succeeded his father, Colonel Miles Brewton, as Powder Receiver. The entrance to the house is on the long side, giving direct access to the stair hall with a door to a reception room facing the street. Features of the exterior of the house are the "carefully executed moulded brick cornice with well defined modillions supporting the overhanging fascia under the eaves." Detroit Publishing Company photograph. Library of Congress.

Church Street south from Tradd, circa 1900-1910. Detroit Publishing Company photograph. Library of Congress.

In February, when James arrived, he was greeted by Owen Wister, the novelist, who became his guide in Charleston. Wister, author of *The Virginian* and the forthcoming Charleston novel *Lady Baltimore,* was the young friend whom James described as "My companion, a Northerner of Southern descent . . . , knew his South in general and his Carolina of that ilk in particular, with an intimacy . . . . He held up for me his bright critical candle, which even in the intrinsic Charleston vividness made its gay flicker, and it was under this aid that, to my extreme convenience, I was able to 'feel' the place."

In Charleston James "found the good society still alive, even if greatly diminished in quantity and activity and even if already becoming tainted in some places by 'the rude Northern contagion.'" He sensed the city's "insidious charm" and in it "the suggestion of a social shrinkage and an economic blight unrepaired." There was "a deficiency of life," a "beauty . . . of other days." The women he saw as "rare, discreet, flitting figures that brushed the garden walls with noiseless skirts in the little melancholy streets of interspaced, overtangled abodes— . . . clad in a rigour of mourning that was like the garb of a conspiracy."

Restoration in Charleston and the country beyond it began eleven years before the Rockefeller family undertook the restoration of Williamsburg, Virginia. But then restoration has been an ongoing process since the first fires and hurricanes began their assault on the city.

In 1916 J. J. Pringle Smith and his wife, the former Heningham Lyons Ellett, began the restoration of Middleton Place, the eighteenth-century plantation twenty miles upriver on the Ashley. In that year the gardens were overgrown and neglected, the lakes and ponds fouled, the ruins of the old manor house covered by the detritus of years.

The west front of the Charleston Hotel on Meeting Street before it was razed in 1960. HABS photograph by Louis I. Schwartz, 1958. Library of Congress.

The Charleston Hotel during the years 1861-1865. This classical façade lent great elegance to Meeting Street until it was razed. Brady-Handy Collection. Library of Congress.

Once Middleton Place had been one of the glories of the Low Country, described by Richard Yeadon in 1857 as being "adorned with the richest productions of the painter's and sculptor's arts . . . . " Yeadon, editor of the *Charleston Daily Courier,* declared: "In its natural and artificial beauty and elegance, Middleton Place comes nearer than any place I have ever seen, in America, to the Italian villas, which I visited, or saw, near Rome."

Eight years later, in 1865, a detachment of Sherman's army occupied the plantation. On February 22 of that year the soldiers ransacked the house, casting what they didn't take on the lawns, and then set the house afire. It burned while the fires of Charleston were still smouldering, and with the destruction of the noble house went over a century of refinement and gracious living.

Portrait, circa 1771, by Benjamin West of Arthur Middleton, his wife Mary Izard and their first child Henry, painted while on a visit to London. On loan to Middleton Place Foundation from Dr. Henry Middleton Drinker. Courtesy, Middleton Place Foundation.

Aerial view of Middleton Place, showing Henry Middleton's garden which he carved out of the wilderness on the banks of the Ashley River. The south flanker can be seen in the upper left. The main axis of the garden runs through the ruins of the main house, the walls of which finally fell during the earthquake of 1886. The butterfly lakes are in the foreground, and the body of water to the left is the rice mill pond. Courtesy, Middleton Place.

South flanker at Middleton Place. Originally built as a gentlemen's guest wing, it offered hospitality to many patriots during the Revolution. In 1781 the terms of surrender of British troops and their withdrawal from South Carolina were accepted at Middleton Place. Courtesy, Middleton Place Foundation.

The story of Middleton Place is a South Carolina saga in the grand tradition. The first Middleton was Edward, who emigrated from England, first to Barbados and then, in 1678, to South Carolina. His son Arthur was president of the convention that, in 1719, overthrew the Lords Proprietors. Henry Middleton (1717-1784), Arthur's son, came into possession of the property in 1741, as part of her dowry when he married Mary Williams, daughter of John Williams, a wealthy landowner. They named the property Middleton Place and at once began a splendid creation of land and water, flowers and trees, rice plantation and self-contained world. Henry was probably the greatest landholder in Carolina—fifty thousand acres that supported approximately eight hundred slaves.

During the years before the Revolution Middleton Place grew to be one of the great estates of America. Henry Middleton envisioned gardens on a grand scale and they were unlike any in the colonies at the time. Classical in concept, geometric in pattern, the gardens featured parterres, vistas, allées, arbors and bowling greens. And everywhere, among the live oaks and Spanish moss, was the water, reflecting in its depths the Carolina skies. Alexander Garden, the Charleston physician and botanist, in 1757 described the *Magnolia grandiflora,* which grows here, as "the finest and most superb evergreen tree that this earth produced." And in 1786 André Michaux, the French botanist, visited Middleton Place, bringing with him the first camellias *(Camellia japonica)* to be planted in an American garden. Three years later the Duc de la Rochefoucauld, witnessing the accomplishments of almost a half century, praised the garden's beauty.

Henry's son Arthur (1742-1787), signer of the Declaration of Independence, brought to his home a connoisseur's eye and a cultural appreciation of all beauty. English educated, he and his wife Mary Izard traveled widely on the continent and in 1764 settled in at Middleton Place. When Charleston fell to the British in 1780, Arthur was imprisoned in St. Augustine. In 1781 the terms for surrender of the British troops and their withdrawal from South Carolina were accepted at Middleton Place.

Their descendants—Henry (1770-1846) and Williams (1809-1883)—occupied the plantation until its destruction at the end of the Civil War. Henry served for ten years in both houses in the state legislature, was governor of South Carolina and America's first minister to Russia. Williams, named for his great-grandmother, was intensely interested in rice culture and carried out agricultural and scientific experiments on the property. It was he who introduced the azalea

House at 61 Washington Street. This 1930 photograph shows the condition many fine old houses were in before restoration was undertaken. Frances B. Johnston photograph. Library of Congress.

(*Azalea indica*) to the gardens. He was one of the signers of the Ordinance of Secession and after the destruction of his home, with financial aid from his sister Eliza Middleton Fisher of Philadelphia, he continued his ownership during the era of Reconstruction, when many Southern families were forced to relinquish their homes.

Before the earthquake of 1886, the south flanker built as a gentlemen's guest wing, the surviving segment of the original house, was roofed over and strengthened. The earthquake itself accomplished what Sherman's torch could not: the standing walls, bleak against the sky, tumbled and only a pile of scattered bricks, covered over by thirty years undergrowth, remained when the Smiths (he was a descendant of the Middletons) began the arduous task of restoring Middleton Place.

By the 1920's the south flanker was again restored. Now, beautifully appointed with furniture, silver, china, paintings and books, it glows with all the beauty of the eighteenth century.

Dr. Joseph Glover House, 81 Rutledge Avenue. This residence illustrates the size and spaciousness of many Charleston residences. The door to the street is a typical Charleston entrance. HABS photograph by Louis I. Schwartz, 1963. Library of Congress.

At numbers 89 and 91 Church Street, a neighbor of the Heyward-Washington House, and just opposite the home of Theodosia Burr Alston, stand two buildings which, while not in the true sense a literary shrine, evoke strong feelings in the hearts of visitors to Charleston.

A narrow passage in the center leads to a courtyard beyond. This is Cabbage Row, the setting of DuBose Heyward's novel *Porgy* (1925). Sam Smalls, the prototype of Porgy, was a cripple who traveled about the city in his goat cart and was called "Goat Sammy." Heyward noticed an article in the *News and Courier* concerning Sam, who had shot another man over a woman. This brief account became the germ of an idea. The result was the novel which was said to be "the first novel written about the character of an American Negro which was at once true to life and a work of art."

Scene at Market Street and East Bay after the tornado of 1938. Works Projects Administration photograph in the National Archives.

Fish peddler in the years before World War I. Peddlers were familiar sights on the streets and many of their cries became part of the background music of Charleston. New York Public Library Picture Collection.

Heyward named his character Porgy for a fish sold on the streets of Charleston. The fish seller's cry was:

> *Porgy walk, Porgy talk,*
> *Porgy eat with a knife and fork.*

It is unlikely that DuBose Heyward ever knew Sam Smalls, who died in the 1930's, although almost every one in Charleston had at one time seen him in his goat cart. Before her death his mother, Elvira Gibbs, said of Sam, one of her twenty-seven children: "Sam was a cripple. He fell sick when he was a little child. He had feet but was unable to walk. One arm was bad, too. But he had a strong body and a strong voice."

Heyward gave the voice speech in the novel, and later in

View from the roof of the Dock Street Theatre, showing the path of the tornado of 1938 and the damage that resulted. Works Project Administration photograph in the National Archives.

the play produced by the Theatre Guild. George Gershwin brought song to Porgy's lips in 1935, when the play became the opera *Porgy and Bess*. The tenement on Church Street has been restored and today two shops flank the entrance to the courtyard, one called "Porgy," the other "Bess." The opera with its enduring melodies has carried Charleston's name to the far corners of the earth.

ALTHOUGH Charleston before World War II was an important port, the city like much of America suffered an economic depression between the wars. Wealthy northerners bought up Low Country plantations and restored them, but Charleston in the 1930's was far removed from the elegant city we observe today.

Restoration at that time was restricted to a few buildings which, by their appearance, became small oases to be admired and cherished. Yet Charleston, despite its lack of wealth, always retained its elegance. There were those householders who somehow managed to see the houses were painted, the gardens kept as they should be.

In the 1930's the Dock Street Theatre, one of the earliest restorations, emerged from the shell of the Planters' Hotel at 135 Church Street.

At the war's end the Historic Charleston Foundation was founded (1947), its principal concern area rehabilitation and the stabilization of historic areas throughout the city. In a little over three decades the face of the city has changed, one of America's most cherished architectural and historic areas preserved and revitalized. The splendor of Charleston today must be seen, otherwise it is difficult to appreciate the magnitude and breadth of the Foundation's accomplishment. Its unique character was instrumental in luring the Spoleto Festival, long successful in Italy, in 1977 to the New World for the first of its annual appearances in Charleston.

The old historic area, the charm of Rainbow Row or Ansonborough reflect this as do those homes on the Battery which the novelist Josephine Pinckney characterized as "classic porticoes next door to opulent bay windows, the linear spirit of Greece reproving the bulges of Victorian taste."

Charleston has survived, and Charleston has endured. And Charleston is, as Samuel Gaillard Stoney wrote, "in the end preeminently herself." Her story has been twice told, oft told, and will be again. It is one that must, almost begin "once upon a time," or as John Bennett wrote in *Doctor to the Dead*:

A long time ago, befo' yestidy was bo'n,
an' befo' bygones was uster-bes.

A turn of the century view of Stoll's Alley near the Battery. The Trezevant House, one of the oldest in the city, is shown here. Print and Picture Department, Free Library of Philadelphia.

Stoll's Alley Shop. Compare this with the earlier photograph of this charming street before it was restored. Frances B. Johnston photograph, circa 1930. Library of Congress.

Bibliography

Adams, Alexander B. *John James Audubon.* New York: G. P. Putnam's Sons, 1966.

Barzman, Sol. *Madmen and Geniuses. The Vice-Presidents of the United States.* Chicago: Follett Publishing Company, 1974.

Beauvallet, Léon. *Rachel and the New World. A Trip to the United States and Cuba.* New York: Dix, Edwards & Company, 1856.

Becker, Carl. *The Declaration of Independence: A Study in History of Political Ideas.* New York: Alfred A. Knopf, 1964.

Bowen, Catherine Drinker. *Miracle at Philadelphia.* Boston: An Atlantic Monthly Press Book, Little Brown and Company, 1966.

Bridenbaugh, Carl. *Cities in the Wilderness: Urban Life in America, 1625-1742.* New York: Capricorn Books, 1955.

———. *Cities in Revolt: Urban Life in America, 1743-1776.* New York: Alfred A. Knopf, 1955.

Burton, E. Milby. *The Siege of Charleston, 1861-1865.* Columbia: University of South Carolina Press, 1970.

City of Charleston Yearbook, 1886. Charleston: Walker, Evans & Cogswell Company, 1886.

Dwight, C. Harrison. "Count Rumford: His Majesty's Colonel in Carolina," *The South Carolina Historical Magazine,* Volume LVII, No. 1 (January, 1956).

Ford, Alice (ed.). *Audubon By Himself.* Garden City: The Natural History Press (Published for the American Museum of Natural History), 1969.

Heyward, DuBose. *Porgy.* New York: Doubleday & Company, Inc., 1953.

James, Henry. *The American Scene.* Bloomington: Indiana University Press, 1968.

Lander, Ernest McPherson, Jr. *A History of South Carolina, 1865-1960.* Chapel Hill: University of North Carolina Press, 1960.

Lincoln, F. S. *Charleston.* Foreword by E. Milby Burton. New York: Corinthian Publications, Inc., 1946.

Molloy, Robert. *Charleston. A Gracious Heritage.* New York: D. Appleton-Century Company, Inc., 1947.

Its quiet streets and more modest homes have as great an appeal as the great houses.   Marjorie R. Maurer photograph.

Pinckney, Josephine. *Three O'Clock Dinner*. New York: The Viking Press, 1945.

Ravenel, Harriott Hörry. *Eliza Pinckney*. New York: Charles Scribner's Sons, 1896.

Ravenel, Mrs. St. Julien (Harriott Hörry). *Charleston: The Place and the People*. New York: The Macmillan Company, 1906.

Rhett, Robert Goodwyn. *Charleston: An Epic of Carolina*. Richmond: Garrett and Massie, Incorporated, 1940.

Robertson, E. Arnot. *The Spanish Town Papers*. London: The Cresset Press, 1959.

St. Clair, William. *Trelawny. The Incurable Romancer*. New York: The Vanguard Press, 1978.

Sass, Herbert Ravenel. "The Charleston Story," *Charleston Grows*. Charleston: Carolina Art Association, 1949.

Simons, Albert and Thomas, W. H. Johnson. *An Architectural Guide to Charleston, South Carolina 1700-1900*. Charleston: Historic Charleston Foundation (compiler), 1971.

Stoney, Samuel Gaillard. *Charleston: Azaleas and Old Bricks*. Photographs by Bayard Wootten. Boston: The Riverside Press, Houghton Mifflin Company, Cambridge, 1937.

Verner, Elizabeth O'Neill. *Mellowed By Time*. Columbia: Bostick & Thornley, Inc., 1941.

Whitelaw, Robert N. S. and Levkoff, Alice F. *Charleston Come Hell or High Water*. Columbia: R. L. Bryan Company, 1975.

Williams, Frances Leigh. *Plantation Patriot*. New York: Harcourt, Brace & World, Inc., 1967.

Wister, Owen. *Lady Baltimore*. New York: The Macmillan Company, 1906.

Zahniser, Marvin R. *Charles Cotesworth Pinckney*. Chapel Hill: University of North Carolina Press (for the Institute of Early American History and Culture at Williamsburg, Virginia), 1967.

Detailing enriches every Charleston structure, be it private home or public building.   Marjorie R. Maurer photograph.

Index

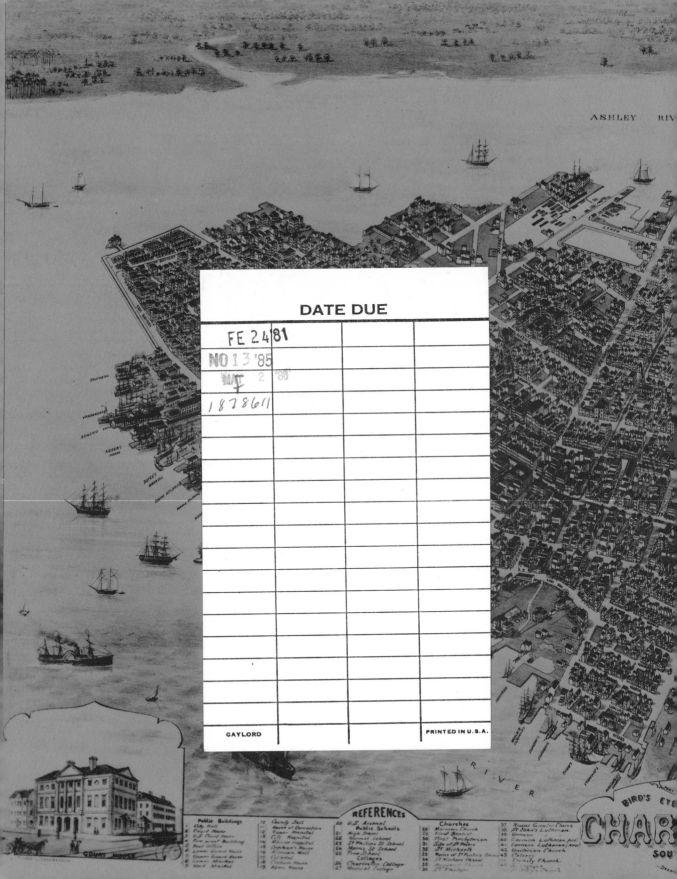

DATE DUE

FE 24 81		
NO 13 '85		
MI 2 '88		
1 8 7 8 6 1 1		
GAYLORD		PRINTED IN U.S.A.